RENAISSANCE

VOLUME 5

Guilds and Crafts — Landscape Painting

GROLIER
EDUCATIONAL

Published by Grolier Educational
Sherman Turnpike
Danbury, Connecticut 06816

Set ISBN 0-7172-5673-1
Volume 5 ISBN 0-7172-5667-7

Library of Congress Cataloging-in-Publication Data

Renaissance.
    p. cm.
Summary: Chronicles the cultural and artistic flowering
known as the Renaissance that flourished in Europe and
in other parts of the world from approximately 1375 to
1575 A.D.
Includes index.
Contents: v. 1. Africa–Bologna — v. 2. Books and libraries–
Constantinople — v. 3. Copernicus–Exploration — v. 4.
Eyck–Government — v. 5. Guilds and crafts–Landscape
painting — v. 6. Language–Merchants — v. 7. Michelangelo–
Palaces and villas — v. 8. Palestrina–Reformation — v. 9.
Religious dissent–Tapestry — v. 10. Technology–Zwingli.
  ISBN 0-7172-5673-1 (set : alk. paper)
  1. Renaissance—Juvenile literature. [1. Renaissance.]
I. Grolier Educational (Firm)
  CB361 .R367 2002
  940.2'1—dc21
                        2002002477

For information address the publisher:
Grolier Educational, Sherman Turnpike,
Danbury, Connecticut 06816

FOR BROWN PARTWORKS

Project Editor: Shona Grimbly
Deputy Editor: Rachel Bean
Text Editor: Chris King
Designer: Sarah Williams
Picture Research: Veneta Bullen
Maps: Colin Woodman
Design Manager: Lynne Ross
Production: Matt Weyland
Managing Editor: Tim Cooke
Consultant: Stephen A. McKnight
                         University of Florida

Printed and bound in Singapore

ABOUT THIS BOOK

This is one of a set of 10 books that tells the story of the Renaissance—a time of discovery and change in the world. It was during this period—roughly from 1375 to 1575—that adventurous mariners from Europe sailed the vast oceans in tiny ships and found the Americas and new sea routes to the Spice Islands of the East. The influx of gold and silver from the New World and the increase in trade made many merchants and traders in Europe extremely rich. They spent some of their wealth on luxury goods like paintings and gold and silver items for their homes, and this created a new demand for the work of artists of all kinds. Europe experienced a cultural flowering as great artists like Leonardo da Vinci, Michelangelo, and Raphael produced masterpieces that have never been surpassed.

At the same time, scholars were rediscovering the works of the ancient Greek and Roman writers, and this led to a new way of looking at the world based on observation and the importance of the individual. This humanism, together with other new ideas, spread more rapidly than ever before thanks to the development of printing with movable type.

There was upheaval in the church too. Thinkers such as Erasmus and Luther began to question the teachings of the established church, and this eventually led to a breakaway from the Catholic church and the setting up of Protestant churches—an event called the Reformation.

The set focuses on Europe, but it also looks at how societies in other parts of the world such as Africa, China, India, and the Americas were developing, and the ways in which the Islamic and Christian worlds interacted.

The entries in this set are arranged alphabetically and are illustrated with paintings, photographs, drawings, and maps, many from the Renaissance period. Each entry ends with a list of cross-references to other entries in the set, and at the end of each book there is a timeline to help you relate events to one another in time.

There is also a useful "Further Reading" list that includes websites, a glossary of special terms, and an index covering the whole set.

Contents

Volume 5

Guilds and Crafts

In the late Middle Ages and the Renaissance guilds provided the basic framework for economic activity. They were professional associations organized to protect the commercial interests of their members and to regulate the quality of their goods and services.

Guilds grew up in towns where trade and crafts were centered; people in different professions, like merchants, doctors, lawyers, craftsmen, and artists, belonged to different guilds. Because they were so important in regulating economic activity guilds often played an important role in town governments. They were also central to the social lives of their community, organizing festivities and processions.

Guilds emerged in western Europe around the 11th century, when relative religious and political stability led to the growth of trade, communications, and towns. Merchants, who had previously been little more than traveling peddlers, began to establish trading networks within their own countries and also across the length and breadth of Europe. They banded together to protect themselves from robberies as they traveled around, and these associations soon developed into the first guilds.

PROFESSIONAL GUILDS

Gradually, merchants based themselves in the growing towns and cities that provided the main markets for their products, and they began to delegate activities such as transporting and producing goods to other people. Their guilds became highly organized in order to protect their trading interests. Guilds had a monopoly on local trade and often controlled certain aspects of international trade as well. Seeing the effectiveness of the merchant guilds, other professionals such as bankers, lawyers, and doctors also began to form their own guilds.

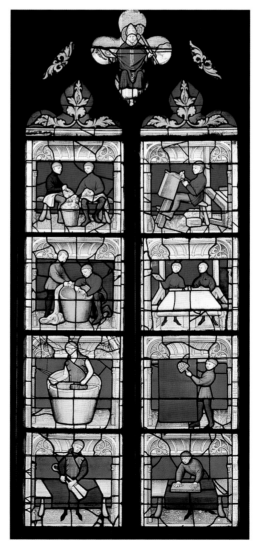

Left: This 15th-century stained-glass window in a French church was paid for by the local drapers' guild. Drapers were cloth merchants, and the window shows all the stages involved in processing and finishing cloth.

Above: A 15th-century illustration showing a procession of the guild of lawyers in Perugia, Italy. Guilds organized many processions and festivities, providing a focus for their local communities.

were made by skilled craftsmen working in their own workshops. The production of items such as textiles involved many stages and many skilled workers. For example, transforming raw wool into a fine garment involved numerous steps. The wool had to be cleaned and spun; the thread then had to be woven into cloth; the cloth had to be softened (fulled) and dyed; and last, it had to be cut and sewn to make clothes. Different craftsmen specialized in each stage of the process. At first the merchant and professional guilds tended to oppose the formation of craft associations. However, by the mid-15th century craftsmen were well represented on the town councils of a large number of urban centers.

STRONG AND WEAK

Nevertheless, some guilds were more powerful than others, and tensions often arose. In Florence, for example, the guilds of bankers and money-changers, lawyers and judges, doctors and pharmacists, silk workers, and merchants—known as the *arti maggiori*, or "greater guilds"—had much more political influence than those of poorer craftsmen such as textile workers. This balance of power changed briefly in 1378, when the woolcarders, or *ciompi* (people who processed wool before it was spun into thread), took part in a rebellion that gave the "minor guilds" a dominant role in the city government—although the major guilds recovered their power a few years later.

Crafts were centered around family workshops, and training was regulated by guilds. Each workshop was owned and run by a master, who was qualified in his own trade. He was helped by assistants, who were also qualified, and apprentices. Apprentices were boys

By the 12th century these guildsmen had become some of the wealthiest inhabitants of towns. They exercised a powerful influence on town councils, particularly in the cities of Flanders (present-day Belgium and parts of the Netherlands and France) and northern Italy. Because they had played a key part in the growth of many prosperous commercial centers, when some of these cities became self-governing city-states, the guilds and their members often dominated their governments.

CRAFT GUILDS

The merchant and professional guilds were so successful in protecting and advancing their economic and political interests that craftsmen were motivated to organize similar associations. Unlike today, when most goods are produced in factories, in the Renaissance they who had been sent by their families to learn a craft. In return for often quite large sums of money masters took apprentices into their houses and provided them with food, clothing, and training. Apprentices usually trained for between five and nine years. When

> *Craft guilds controlled production by establishing very exacting standards and fixed charges for work*

their training was complete, they became "journeymen," who could be hired to work by the day. Journeymen could become masters by producing a "masterpiece," an outstanding piece of work that demonstrated their technical accomplishment. This system of training and working was overseen by a craft guild. The guilds themselves were run by associations of masters, although control lay in the hands of a small number of officials and advisers. They set the standards for workmanship and materials, and determined how to protect their members from cheap imports from other towns.

GUILD INTERESTS AND CONTROLS

In the cities where the craft guilds had influence, they controlled production by establishing very exacting standards and fixed charges for work. While this practice guaranteed high standards of production, it restricted competition and discouraged innovation. Moreover, guild members found it in their economic interest to limit the number of people who were qualified to practice their trades. So they restricted the number of apprentices whom master craftsmen could train. They also exploited journeymen, who were often highly skilled, by limiting their pay and making it difficult for them to become established masters with their own workshops. Membership in a guild eventually became more a matter of

Below: This picture is part of a 15th-century sign for a Venetian silk weaver. It shows a typical workshop, with one man spinning silk into thread and another weaving it into cloth on a loom.

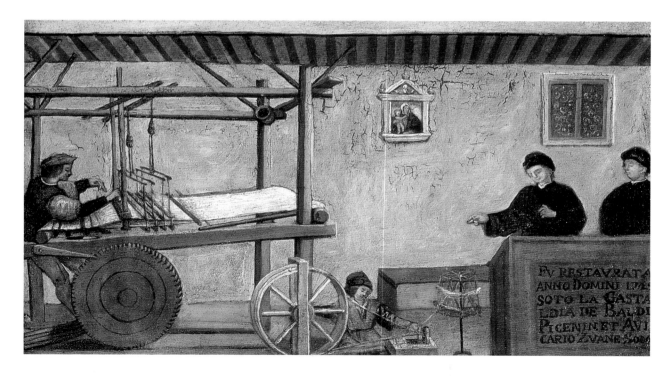

PATRONS OF THE ARTS

Guilds spent large sums of money commissioning buildings, paintings, and sculptures to beautify the towns and cities in which they were based. In doing so, they expressed their wealth and power to neighboring towns, and individual guilds competed with each other to commission the most up-to-date and impressive works of art. As major patrons of the arts, guilds were instrumental in providing an environment in which the artistic developments of the Renaissance could flourish. For example, in the Italian city of Florence, which was an early center of the Renaissance, guilds were the most important patrons of the arts throughout the 15th century. The Guild of Wool Workers paid for statues to decorate the doorway of the cathedral, and the Guild of Cloth Importers commissioned the sculptor Ghiberti to create two sets of bronze doors for the baptistery of the cathedral. Each guild also commissioned a sculpture of its patron saint to decorate the outside of the Orsanmichele, a guild building that had a church on the ground floor and a granary above. All the leading sculptors of the day, including Ghiberti and Donatello, produced statues for the Orsanmichele.

As well as these large-scale commissions, guilds also paid for numerous more modest works of art to beautify local neighborhoods and buildings. They included altarpieces, paintings, and stained-glass windows in churches, and shrines and drinking fountains in the streets.

Above: A Florentine sculpture that was paid for by the Guild of Masons and Carpenters, whose symbols are shown along the bottom of the frame.

inheritance than a demonstration of skill in a particular craft, as workshops were handed down from father to son.

Guildsmen considered themselves to be upstanding citizens who were committed to their municipalities. For many of them public service was an obligation that they gladly accepted. Guilds were certainly more than economic and political institutions that only promoted the self-interests of their members. They were often closely tied to parishes within towns and cities because professionals and craftsmen who practiced the same trade tended to cluster together in the same area. They involved themselves with charitable activities such as caring for the poor, as well as with the sponsorship of public events such as memorials, parades, festivals, feasts, and competitions to increase the sense of community. They were also some of the most important patrons of art in the Renaissance.

Hapsburg Family

The house of Hapsburg was one of Europe's most powerful royal families. The Hapsburgs held the title Holy Roman emperor for hundreds of years and also ruled territory in Spain, the Netherlands, and Italy. They reached the height of their power during the reign of Charles V (1500–1558).

The Hapsburg family took their name from Habichtsburg, or "Hawk's Castle," where they lived from about 1020. The castle was located in the north of present-day Switzerland. By the end of the 11th century the family had gained lands around Lake Lucerne and was using the title count of Hapsburg.

The lands of the Hapsburgs formed part of the Holy Roman Empire, a loose grouping of duchies, counties, and kingdoms under the nominal control of an emperor. The emperor was elected by his fellow rulers, although he did not officially hold the title until he was crowned by the pope. The first Hapsburg emperor was Rudolf I (1218–1291), who was elected in 1273. A year later Rudolf defeated a rival king, Ottaker II of Bohemia, in battle, seizing the duchy of Austria. It was to remain under Hapsburg rule for over 600 years.

The Hapsburgs lost the imperial crown in 1308, when Rudolf's son Albert was murdered by his own nephew. By now they had also lost their original lands in Switzerland, and for the rest of the 14th century they concentrated on expanding their Austrian territories. The new head of

the family, Duke Rudolf IV, had a great influence on the city of Vienna. In 1359 he rebuilt the 200-year-old church of Saint Stephen's, transforming it into a stunning cathedral. Six years later he enhanced the status of the city even further when he founded a university there. It was the first university in the German-speaking world.

Above: The Holy Roman emperor Frederick III, who was crowned in 1452. He was the last emperor to be crowned by the pope in Rome.

The Hapsburgs regained the imperial throne in 1438. The head of the family and duke of Austria was then Albert V (1397–1439), who was married to the daughter of the Holy Roman emperor Sigismund. On his father-in-law's death Albert became king of Hungary and was soon elected emperor as Albert II. He immediately introduced administrative reforms to help bring stability to the empire. However, Albert's reign was cut short when he died during a campaign against the Ottoman Turks.

FREDERICK III

Albert was succeeded by his cousin Frederick III (1415–1493), who was elected in 1440 but not officially crowned until 12 years later. Frederick

---

Frederick's motto was "Austria is destined to rule the world"

---

was the last emperor to be crowned by the pope in Rome. He is famous for his motto, which was made up of the five vowels A.E.I.O.U. They supposedly stood for the Latin phrase *Austriae est imperare orbi universo* ("Austria is destined to rule the world") or the German phrase *Alles Erdreich ist Österreich untertan* ("The whole world is subject to Austria").

The two mottoes exaggerate the strength of the Hapsburgs at the time of Frederick's reign. During his rule the family lost control of Hungary, Bohemia, and even parts of Austria. However, one act by Frederick did much to restore the family's power. In 1477 he arranged for his son Max-

imilian (1459–1519) to marry Mary of Burgundy. It has been called the most important marriage in the history of Europe because it gave later members of the Hapsburg family territories in the Low Countries and France, making them a major western European power.

Maximilian succeeded Frederick as emperor in 1493. He was extremely ambitious and wanted to rule over a united empire of western Europe in the

Below: Saint Stephen's Cathedral in Vienna, which was built in the 14th century by Duke Rudolf IV of Austria, a member of the Hapsburg family. Rudolf also founded the city's university.

Below: Emperor Maximilian II, who ruled the Hapsburgs' Austrian lands while his cousin Philip II reigned in Spain.

same way as Charlemagne had almost 700 years earlier. He tried to achieve this with a mixture of political treaties, military force, and above all, family marriages. Maximilian's ability to gain territory through peaceful means led to the popular saying: "Let others wage war; you, fortunate Austria, marry."

Maximilian regained control over his family's traditional lands in Austria, some of which had been seized by

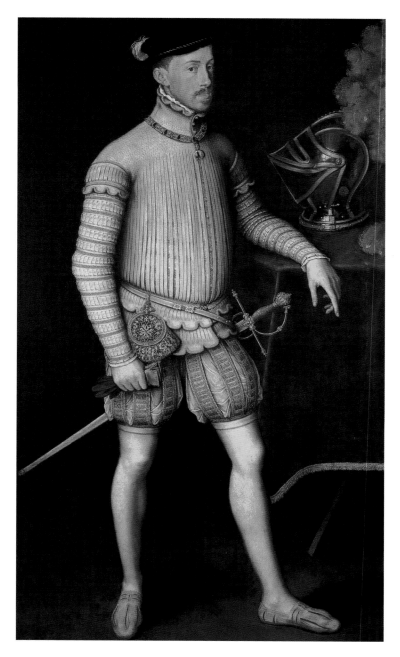

Hungary during his father's reign. Then he waged war against Bohemia and secured a treaty by which Bohemian and Hungarian territory would later pass to the Hapsburgs. After his wife died in a hunting accident, Maximilian defended the lands in the Low Countries, which his family had inherited from her. Most importantly, he married his son Philip to the Spanish princess Joanna, daughter of Ferdinand and Isabella of Aragon and Castile. Philip died in 1506, but by then all the male heirs of the Spanish monarchs were also dead. The Spanish lands passed to Joanna and through her to her Hapsburg sons, Charles and Ferdinand (1503–1564).

CHARLES V

When Maximilian died in 1519, he was succeeded by his grandson Charles V, who became emperor at the age of 19.

Charles V used silver from the Americas to fund wars in Europe

---

As well as controlling all the European lands belonging to the Hapsburgs, Charles had access to the new Spanish colonies in the Americas. Charles received a tremendous amount of silver and other treasure from America, which he used to fund wars on the borders of his European empire.

Despite their great wealth and power, the Hapsburgs constantly had to fight to defend their lands. In western Europe France and Spain were often at war, a situation that was made worse by the personal hatred between Charles V and Francis I of France. In the east the

Hapsburgs' lands, on the very edge of Christendom, were threatened by the advance of the powerful Ottoman Turks—in 1529 the Ottomans unsuccessfully laid seige to Vienna itself. In Germany, meanwhile, the religious upheavals caused by the Protestant Reform- ation placed Charles, who was Catholic, in conflict with many of the regional princes who owed allegiance to him.

THE EMPIRE DIVIDES

It was during Charles' reign that the Hapsburg empire split in two. In 1522 he allowed his younger brother Ferdinand to take over the family's Austrian lands. Shortly before his death Charles gave his Spanish lands to his son Philip (1527–1598), who became Philip II of Spain. This division had a lasting effect on the political history of Europe, since Ferdinand's descendants ruled the Holy Roman Empire while Philip's descendants reigned in Spain.

Ferdinand was elected Holy Roman emperor in 1558. Unlike Charles, Ferdinand was eager to find a compromise with the Protestant princes. In the final years of his brother's reign Ferdinand took part in the Diet (or assembly) of Augsburg. There he signed an agreement on the emperor's behalf that allowed regional rulers to decide the religion of their subjects. Ferdinand also agreed to pay tribute to the Ottoman Turks. Through concessions such as these Ferdinand managed to bring stability to the Hapsburg lands.

Above: This dish shows the coronation of Emperor Charles V, under whose rule the Hapsburgs reached the height of their power.

SEE ALSO

♦ Americas
♦ Bohemia
♦ Charles V
♦ Elizabeth I
♦ Francis I
♦ Germany
♦ Holy Roman Empire
♦ Maximilian I
♦ Netherlands
♦ Philip II
♦ Protestantism
♦ Reformation
♦ Spain

Despite his tolerant attitude toward his Protestant opponents, Ferdinand remained a strong supporter of Cath- olicism. His eldest son Maximilian II had more com- plicated religious views and was sympathetic to the ideas of Martin Luther in his youth. He was threatened with disinheritance by his father and afterward agreed to outwardly support the Catholic faith. However, he took many steps to promote religious tolerance within the empire. In contrast, Maximilian's cousin Philip II of Spain spent much of his reign waging religious wars and trying to suppress revolts in the Protestant Netherlands. He also sent a great Armada (or fleet) against England, although this enterprise ended in disaster when many of the ships were destroyed.

For centuries the Hapsburgs had acquired territory by marrying into other noble houses. Unsurprisingly, they were eager to prevent rival families from gaining Hapsburg lands in the same way. From the 16th century they increasingly married within their own family. For example, Philip II took his cousin Maximilian's daughter Anna as his fourth wife. Maximilian, mean- while, married his own cousin Maria. This tendency to intermarry, however, led to problems of infertility, and the Spanish Hapsburg line died out by the end of the 17th century. The Austrian Hapsburgs continued to hold the title of Holy Roman emperor until 1806, when the empire was dissolved.

Left: This portrait of Henry VIII is by Hans Holbein the Younger. Holbein was Henry's official court painter— during his time in England he painted portraits of many of the country's most important figures.

Henry VIII

The second Tudor king of England, Henry VIII (1491–1547) was the son of King Henry VII and Elizabeth of York. His older brother Arthur died in 1502; and when his father also died seven years later, Henry became king at the age of 17. He immediately married his brother's widow, Catherine of Aragon, the daughter of Ferdinand and Isabella of Spain.

At the time that Henry came to the throne, Spain was one of two powers that dominated Europe. The other was France, and in 1512 Henry joined forces with his father-in-law, Ferdinand II of Aragon, in a war against the French. The following year he captured the French towns of Thérouanne and Tournai, and won the battle of Guinegate, also known as the Battle of the Spurs because so many French horsemen lost their spurs in the retreat.

While the young king engaged in military adventures in continental Europe, he allowed the day-to-day running of the country to be carried out by his chief adviser, Thomas Wolsey (about 1475–1530). The son of a butcher, Wolsey rose to a position of great power, becoming lord chancellor

---

Henry's adviser Thomas Wolsey made many enemies among the nobility

---

as well as a cardinal and the archbishop of York. Wolsey used these positions to build up a great amount of personal wealth. In doing so, however, he made many enemies, especially among the nobility, who resented him because of his lowly birth.

ANNE BOLEYN

In 1522 Henry's reign was transformed by the arrival at court of a young maid of honor—Anne Boleyn. By now Henry had been married for 13 years, yet he had no son. A daughter, Mary, had been born in 1516, but five other children had either died at birth or shortly afterward. Henry desperately needed a male heir and, convinced that Catherine could not provide him with one, began to look elsewhere.

The beautiful young courtier Anne Boleyn provided the king with a

potential solution to his problems. Henry fell in love with her soon after her arrival at court, but knew that he would have to find a reason to divorce Catherine before he could marry Anne. In 1527 he ordered Wolsey to ask Pope Clement VII to annul, or cancel, his marriage. Wolsey argued that the marriage was unlawful because Catherine was Henry's brother's widow.

Unfortunately for Henry, he could not have chosen a worse time to ask the pope for help. Clement could not risk offending the powerful Holy Roman emperor Charles V, who was Catherine's nephew. Knowing that Charles was opposed to it, the pope continually refused to approve the divorce. Wolsey's failure to get Henry's marriage annulled led to his downfall. The

Below: Anne Boleyn, the second wife of Henry VIII. In order to marry Anne, Henry was forced to make a break from the Catholic church in Rome.

SPLENDOR AND STATUS

Henry VIII saw himself as the equal of European monarchs like Francis I of France and Charles V, the Holy Roman emperor and king of Spain, and believed that his palaces should reflect his status. Royal residences such as Whitehall Palace, Windsor Castle, and Hampton Court were some of the most spectacular in Europe. The most famous of these palaces is probably Hampton Court, situated on the Thames River outside London. Work on the building was begun by the Lord Chancellor Thomas Wolsey in 1515. Wolsey had intended to live there himself, but he gave it to the king in 1525.

Henry then spent thousands of pounds rebuilding and extending the palace, employing artists and craftsmen from all over Europe. For example, the Great Hall was decorated by tapestries woven with silver and gold thread made by the Flemish weaver Willem Kampeneer. The most famous artist to work at Henry's court, however, was the German painter Hans Holbein. Holbein's full-length portrait of Henry presents an image of the king that is still familiar today.

Above: The entrance to Hampton Court, the favorite palace of Henry VIII given to him by Thomas Wolsey in 1525.

cardinal's enemies managed to turn the king against him, and he was stripped of all his titles.

Henry was now in an extremely awkward position. Without the pope's cooperation he could not marry Anne. However, a solution to the dilemma was found by Thomas Cromwell (about 1485–1540), who had replaced Wolsey as Henry's most trusted adviser. He proposed that the English church should separate from Rome so that it could grant Henry a divorce.

At the time of Henry's reign there was much religious turmoil in Europe. In 1517 the German monk Martin Luther had openly challenged both the

---

Cromwell proposed that the English church should split from Rome

---

authority of the pope and many established church teachings. Henry was fiercely opposed to Luther's beliefs —in 1521 he had written a book attacking Lutheranism. However, in order to produce a male heir, the king was forced to make a similar break from papal control.

THE ENGLISH REFORMATION

The establishment of a separate Church of England was not achieved in a single step, but instead was the result of a long, drawn-out parliamentary process that gradually weakened the church's power over the king. It began in 1529 and reached a climax in November 1534 with the Act of Supremacy, which declared that Henry was the supreme head of the Church of England. Later, in a process known as the dissolution of the monasteries, Henry confiscated all of the church's property and wealth.

In the meantime Henry had finally married Anne Boleyn in 1533. His previous marriage had been annulled by the new archbishop of Canterbury, Thomas Cranmer. Anne was already pregnant at the time of her wedding. However, rather than the son that Henry wished for, she bore him a daughter, Elizabeth. The king hoped that a son would soon follow, but two pregnancies resulted in a miscarriage and a stillborn child. By 1536 Henry had grown tired of Anne and, suspecting that she was being unfaithful to him, had her sent to the Tower of London. She was tried for treason, found guilty, and beheaded.

Just 11 days after the execution of Anne Henry married Jane Seymour, who had served as a lady-in-waiting to his first two wives. She succeeded in producing a male heir, Edward, but died shortly afterward. Three years later the king married a German princess, Anne of Cleves, for political reasons. Henry had seen a sketch of his future fourth wife by the court painter Hans Holbein, but was disappointed when he actually met her. He did not like her appearance and is said to have nicknamed her the "Flanders mare." The marriage lasted only a short time before it was annulled.

FINAL YEARS

In the last years of his reign Henry began to act in an increasingly tyrannical fashion. Cromwell, who had engineered the king's disastrous fourth marriage, was executed in 1540. He was just one of many important figures to meet their deaths as Henry became more and more suspicious of those around him. Some noblemen were

killed simply because they had royal blood and could possibly make a claim to the throne in the future.

Henry married twice more. His fifth wife was Catherine Howard, the 20-year-old granddaughter of the Duke of Norfolk. Catherine had several affairs behind the king's back after she was married and was beheaded in 1542. The king's final marriage in 1543 was to the quiet and loyal Catherine Parr, who remained Henry's wife until his death in January 1547. For much of the final period of his life Henry was extremely sick, yet he still found enough energy to wage a costly war with France.

All three of Henry's children ruled England after his death. He was succeeded by Edward VI, his son by Jane Seymour, who was followed in turn by Mary I and Elizabeth I.

Above: Henry VIII with his lord chancellor Thomas Wolsey. Wolsey was Henry's chief adviser during the early part of his reign, but eventually fell from favor.

SEE ALSO

♦ Elizabeth I
♦ England
♦ Holbein
♦ More, Thomas
♦ Protestantism
♦ Reformation

Holbein

Hans Holbein (1497–1543) was the outstanding German artist of his generation and enjoyed international success, working first in the Swiss city Basel and later as court painter to the English king Henry VIII. He excelled as a portrait painter and created some of the most lifelike and powerful images of courtiers and royalty of the Renaissance.

Holbein was born in Augsburg, southern Germany, and trained in the workshop of his father, who was a painter. He then moved to Basel in Switzerland, which was a major center of learning and publishing. There Holbein produced book illustrations, portraits, religious pictures, mural decorations for houses, and designs for stained glass. He soon became the leading artist in the city. However, he left in 1526, when Basel became a center of religious unrest between Catholics and Protestants.

MOVE TO ENGLAND

With the encouragement of the Dutch scholar Erasmus, whose portrait he painted three times, Holbein moved to England, which was prosperous and stable under the rule of King Henry VIII. Erasmus had visited England on several occasions and had influential friends there, including the statesman Thomas More. Holbein lodged in More's house when he arrived in London and painted a portrait of his host, which is typical of his style. The face is painted with meticulous detail, from the lines around More's eyes to the glistening stubble on his chin. His importance is emphasized by the sumptuous clothes he wears, Holbein capturing the sheen of the red velvet sleeves, the softness of the robe's fur lining, and the grandeur of the gold chain of royal office.

Holbein soon became successful in England, but in 1528 he returned to Basel, probably because he risked losing his citizen's rights there if he stayed away too long. He remained there four years; but as the religious strife worsened, he returned to England

Below: Holbein's Portrait of Thomas More (1527). This picture was one of the first portraits Holbein painted after his arrival in England in 1526.

in 1532. By this time Thomas More had fallen from royal favor, and Holbein looked elsewhere for patronage. He painted some of his most exceptional portraits at this time, with an eye to attracting the attention of the king. The most magnificent and complex of these paintings is *The Ambassadors* (1533), a double portrait of Jean de Dinteville, the French ambassador to England, and his friend Georges de Selve, Bishop

---

Holbein's paintings outshone anything produced by English artists at the time

---

of Lavour, who served on several occasions as a French ambassador. Holbein portrayed the men full length and almost life size. He showed them leaning on a set of shelves covered with a patterned rug and laden with musical and astronomical instruments. These objects suggest the wealth and culture of the ambassadors and enabled Holbein to display his skill. The strange shape in the foreground is a human skull, skillfully distorted so that it looks realistic only when seen close-up from the edge of the picture. It was a reminder of the briefness of life, a common theme in Renaissance art.

PAINTER TO THE KING

Paintings such as this portrait outshone anything produced by English artists at the time, and Holbein soon attracted the attention of Henry VIII, who appointed him court painter in 1537. Holbein produced a huge number of portraits of royalty and nobility, including some very sensitive drawings, and created the most

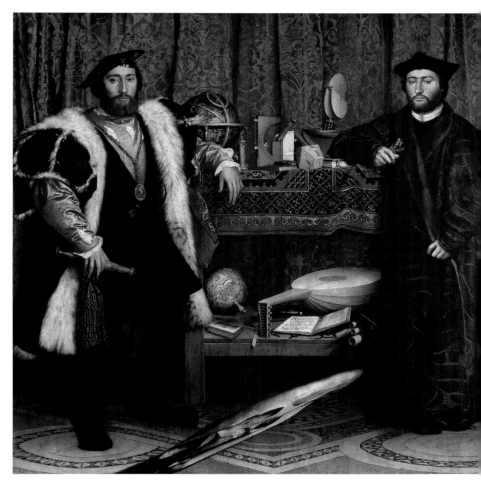

famous—and much copied—images of Henry VIII. These paintings of the king were an important means of projecting the royal image. They included a huge mural for the king's new palace at Whitehall in London, showing the king with Jane Seymour, his third wife, and his parents, Henry VII and Elizabeth of York. Like Holbein's other works for Henry, it celebrated the fame and power of the Tudor dynasty and emphasized the king's strength and elegance. Holbein also produced a wide range of designs for the court, from lavish royal robes and jewelry to bookbindings. He died in 1543, probably from an outbreak of the plague. He had played a key role in shaping the image of the Tudor dynasty and the course of portrait painting.

Above: Holbein's **The Ambassadors,** *painted in 1533. It is one of the largest and most magnificent of his portrait paintings to survive.*

SEE ALSO
♦ German Art
♦ Henry VIII
♦ More, Thomas
♦ Patronage
♦ Portraiture

Holy Roman Empire

Left: The double-headed eagle emblem of the Holy Roman Empire. On the eagle's wings are the individual coats of arms of the various duchies, counties, and principalities that made up the empire.

B ased on present-day Germany, the Holy Roman Empire was one of the strangest institutions in Renaissance Europe. Its head was an emperor, but his power was very limited. The empire was not a state or country in the modern sense, but a collection of hundreds of semi-independent units—principalities, cities, and lands controlled by knights and other noblemen. These regions varied hugely in size and importance.

By the 15th century the emperors had little real control over their most powerful subjects. For convenience these subjects are usually referred to as "the princes," although they actually bore a range of titles, including duke, count, landgrave, and margrave. One,

the ruler of Bohemia, was even a king. The princes also included many ecclesiastical rulers—that is, arch-bishops and bishops who were also great lords governing large territories. The empire was mainly German-speaking and was sometimes referred to as the empire of the German nation. However, it included non-Germans such as the Czechs of Bohemia, and it was not a nation-state.

THE GOLDEN BULL

In 1356 Emperor Charles IV (ruled 1355–1378) issued a document called the Golden Bull that laid down how the empire was to be run. For over a century the princes had elected the emperor, but their decisions had often been disputed. The Golden Bull stated clearly who the electors should be and how they were to carry out their task. From this time onward there was a college of seven electors, consisting of the king of Bohemia, the count Palatine (ruler of the Palatinate in the Rhineland), the duke of Saxony, the margrave of Brandenburg, and three ecclesiastical rulers—the archbishops of Mainz, Trier, and Cologne. They were all important figures, but there were other powerful princes who were not electors, including the rulers of Bavaria, Württemburg, and Hesse.

The fact that they had to be elected was one reason why the emperors had limited powers within the empire.

Before an election the princes could demand, and receive, privileges from the candidates. For this reason an emperor was likely to have made concessions even before he started his reign. This remained true even though from 1438 onward the emperor came from a single family—the Hapsburgs.

HAPSBURG RULE

The Hapsburgs were dukes of Austria, which was in the southeast of the empire, and possessed substantial other German territories. The family's great wealth enabled it to keep hold of the imperial title, often through bribery. All of the Hapsburg emperors,

THE ORIGINS OF THE EMPIRE

The idea of a Holy Roman Empire began during the reign of Charlemagne, the king of the Franks (742–814 A.D.), who conquered much of western Europe. Charlemagne rescued the papacy from its enemies in Italy, and in 800 a grateful Pope Leo III crowned him emperor at Rome. The term Holy Roman emperor was not used until centuries afterward, but the coronation expressed the basic idea that Charlemagne was the legitimate Christian successor to the emperors of ancient Rome.

When Charlemagne died, the empire was divided, and it was over a century before a strong emperor came to power again. Otto I (912–973) reigned over an area that included both Germany and Italy. Otto's successors often clashed with popes over the issue of who should be regarded as the head of the Christian world—Frederick I Barbarossa and Frederick II were among the great emperors involved in such quarrels. In the late 13th century, however, the emperors lost control of Italy, and after that the empire centered on Germany.

Above: Pope Leo III crowns the Frankish king Charlemagne emperor of the Romans in 800. The coronation marked the birth of the idea of the Holy Roman Empire.

especially Charles V, wielded enormous power. However, this power came from the lands that the family held, rather than the title of emperor.

THE REICHSTAG

The emperor's administration had a chancellor at its head and included a treasury and a court of justice. The most important imperial institution was the Diet, or Reichstag, a parliamentlike assembly attended by princes, nobles, and representatives of the towns. In consultation with the emperor it could reach decisions and pass laws. However, it was often the case that neither the Diet nor the emperor could enforce laws if some of the more powerful princes objected.

The lack of a strong central authority in the empire mattered very little when the territories of individual princes were well run. However, it did mean that the empire tended to become smaller as areas close to the frontier were either taken over by

Below: This map shows the extent of the Holy Roman Empire in the early 16th century, as well as some of its most important regions and cities.

powerful neighbors like France or simply broke away. The Swiss cantons (states) were a notable example. They were really independent by the 14th century, although their status was not officially recognized until 1499.

As well as the shrinking of the empire, lack of central political control brought problems of law and order, especially when impoverished nobles and knights misbehaved. Because of such problems there were attempts in the 15th and 16th centuries to reform the government of the empire. However, none of them produced

---

Early Hapsburg rulers often found themselves involved in costly wars

---

results. When the time came for decisions to be put into practice, the princes could not bring themselves to increase the emperor's power at the expense of their own. An alternative plan—a government run by the princes and towns—also proved unworkable.

Early Hapsburg rulers such as Frederick III (ruled 1440–1493) and Maximilian I (ruled 1493–1517) frequently found themselves involved in costly wars over disputed areas of land. Frederick was not a particularly successful soldier and was driven from his ancestral homeland of Austria by Matthias I Corvinus of Hungary. His son Maximilian was at war for much of his reign. He managed to regain Austria and successfully drove the Ottoman Turks from the borders of his lands. However, after an unsuccessful campaign against the powerful Swiss Confederation he was forced to

Holy Roman Empire

BRANDENBURG
POLAND
SAXONY
Cologne HESSE
Trier
Mainz
BOHEMIA
PALATINATE OF THE RHINELAND
FRANCE
WÜRTTEMBURG BAVARIA
Augsburg
AUSTRIA
HUNGARY
SWISS CONFEDERATION

Left: The crown of the Holy Roman emperor, which was made for the coronation of Otto I in 962.

recognize Swiss independence. Wars against France in northern Italy also proved to be failures.

STRENGTH THROUGH MARRIAGE
Although their military campaigns were often unsuccessful, Frederick and Maximilian were able to increase their wealth and power through another means—both managed to create highly important alliances through marriage. As a result, Maximilian's grandson Charles (ruled 1519–1556) inherited Austria, Spain, Spanish America, and the Low Countries. In 1519, after a lavish distribution of bribes, he was elected Holy Roman emperor as Charles V. However, the task of managing and defending his vast territories kept him out of Germany for years at a time, including the vital decade when the Protestant Reformation took hold, increasing the divisions within the empire.

The Reformation was welcomed by many German princes, since it weakened both the pope's and the emperor's power and increased their own. Charles was a great champion of Catholicism, but he was distracted by wars against France and the Ottoman Turks. At last, in 1542 he became free to crush the Protestant princes and assert his authority. However, despite a great victory at Muhlberg in 1547, the opposition of the princes was too much for Charles.

When peace was finally made at the Diet of Augsburg in 1555, the position of the princes was strengthened, since they, and not the emperor, won the right to decide the religion of their subjects. Over the years and centuries that followed, the empire simply became an association of princes. The imperial title continued to bring the Hapsburg emperors both honor and prestige, but not power.

SEE ALSO

♦ Bavaria
♦ Bohemia
♦ Charles V
♦ Free Cities
♦ Germany
♦ Hapsburg Family
♦ Maximilian I
♦ Protestantism
♦ Reformation
♦ Sigismund

Houses

In the Renaissance most of Europe's population consisted of peasants who lived in basic rural houses that had changed little since the Middle Ages. Gradually, however, luxuries that had previously been confined to the palaces and homes of royalty and the nobility began to be used in the houses of more well-to-do farmers and tradesmen.

Throughout Europe houses were built of materials that were locally available. To the south of the Alps stone houses were more common, while to the north timber houses predominated. Most peasants' houses followed the same basic plan; they were rectangular and consisted of two adjoining rooms—a main living area and a sleeping room. Originally the living area was heated by a central fire, which let out its smoke through a hole in the roof as well as into the room. However, by the 16th century masonry (cut-stone) hearths and chimneys were beginning to appear, often located against one of the outer walls of the house. To construct the roof of the house a variety of materials was used: branches covered with leaves and grass, thatch, wooden shingles, clay tiles, and—in the mountainous areas of northern and western Europe—slates and stones.

The basic house plan gradually evolved. Storage areas, reached by a ladder, were created in the roof space, and eventually second, and even third, stories were added. In some parts of

Above: A modern reconstruction of a 15th-century English farmhouse. It has a timber frame and walls made from wattle and daub (woven branches covered with mud, plaster, or cow dung). Behind the fence is a vegetable garden.

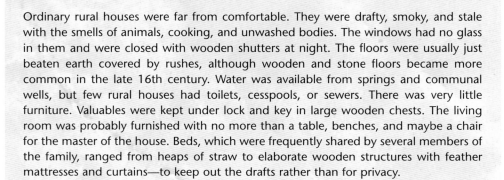

HOME COMFORTS?

Ordinary rural houses were far from comfortable. They were drafty, smoky, and stale with the smells of animals, cooking, and unwashed bodies. The windows had no glass in them and were closed with wooden shutters at night. The floors were usually just beaten earth covered by rushes, although wooden and stone floors became more common in the late 16th century. Water was available from springs and communal wells, but few rural houses had toilets, cesspools, or sewers. There was very little furniture. Valuables were kept under lock and key in large wooden chests. The living room was probably furnished with no more than a table, benches, and maybe a chair for the master of the house. Beds, which were frequently shared by several members of the family, ranged from heaps of straw to elaborate wooden structures with feather mattresses and curtains—to keep out the drafts rather than for privacy.

Europe extensions were added to the first floor that were used to house animals during the winter months. Wealthier farmers elaborated on the basic plan, adding well-furnished rooms, fireplaces, glazed windows, wooden floors, and paneling to create substantial and imposing homes.

TOWN HOUSES

In the increasingly overcrowded towns the plots on which houses were built were considerably smaller than in the country. As a result, town houses were built adjoining each other. They kept the basic rectangular plan, but were built with the narrow end fronting the street. As a result, light was scarce inside, and most urban houses were dark. To create more space—especially since many craftsmen used the second floor as their workshops—town houses extended upward, to as many as four stories. The upper floors stuck out over the narrow streets. At the rear of the house there was a courtyard.

As in the country, building materials depended on the local climate and resources. Houses were constructed of stone, wood, dried clay, or brick. Roofs were tiled, thatched, or covered by flat stones. The windows were fitted with oiled paper or parchment or, for the more fortunate, glass and wooden shutters. Many town houses had their own wells and latrines (toilets).

Houses of prominent tradesmen, merchants, businessmen, and bankers were correspondingly more lavish. Frequently they occupied double plots, which meant that there was much more daylight, and—at the front of the first floor—they boasted a fine "hall" or salon, complete with a large fireplace, polished wooden floors, and carved and decorated wooden paneling. Cellars were used for storage, while the kitchen was situated at the rear of the first floor, next to the back courtyard and the well. Bedrooms, each with their own fireplace, were located on the second and third floors.

Below: A 16th-century painting of a Dutch market place. Typical town houses line the street, and a shop can be seen on the first floor of the house on the left.

Human Form in Art

The portrayal of the unclothed human form (the nude) was central to Italian Renaissance art. Inspired by classical (ancient Greek and Roman) ideas and examples, artists increasingly included nudes in their pictures and sculptures. The ability and skill to depict the human form became a fundamental part of artistic practice, and all apprentices were taught life drawing (drawing a nude model). As artists tried to portray the most beautiful or idealized nudes they could imagine, the skilled depiction of the human body soon became an end in itself.

The portrayal of the nude had been a key theme in the art of ancient Greece and Rome. However, people's attitudes to nudity changed in the early centuries of Christianity. Nakedness was linked with evil, and the naked female form was thought to be particularly evil, because it was Eve who first disobeyed God in the Garden of Eden. Throughout the Middle Ages the only unclothed figures artists could show were Adam and Eve, the baby Jesus, and a stylized image of Christ on the cross.

In 15th-century Italy, when scholars and artists began to study and emulate Greek and Roman art and literature, the unclothed human form once more became a suitable subject for art.

Above: Donatello's statue David, *which was completed around 1440. It was one of the earliest sculpted nudes of the Renaissance.*

Ancient sculptors had tried to portray idealized beauty as part of a wider search for truth, following the writings of the Greek philosopher Plato. In the Renaissance Christian artists came to consider the nude human form, particularly the male form, as a reflection of the divine, since the Bible states that God made humankind in his image.

THEORY AND PRACTICE

Painters and sculptors worked hard to study, understand, and portray the human body. Apprentices began their training by being taught to copy and draw classical sculptures of the human body. They then went on to draw from a living human model in the studio. Life drawing remained an important exercise for artists throughout their careers. Although it was contrary to church teaching, many artists also performed dissections in order to understand the workings of the body better and to see the structure of the bones, muscles, and tissues beneath the skin. Their interest in anatomy paralleled that of doctors, who also carried out dissections.

Artists and theoreticians also searched for rules and formulas that would help them portray the most beautiful human forms possible—nearer to perfection than any living person. They based their ideas on classical writers such as Pliny and Vitruvius. The writer and architect Leon Battista Alberti (1404–1472) thought that artists could portray perfect beauty by applying sets of measurements and proportions to the body that could be expressed as mathematical formulas. Because the circle and square were considered perfect geometrical shapes, artists also tried to relate the human body to them. The best known example is the so-called "Vitruvian man" drawn by Leonardo da Vinci. It is based on the Roman architect Vitruvius's statement that the human body is an ideal form because with outstretched arms and legs it fits into a square and a circle.

A number of classical figure sculptures survived in the Renaissance and had an immense influence on Renaissance painters and sculptors, who viewed them as examples of ideal beauty. The most famous classical sculptures of the male body were the *Apollo Belvedere*, the *Belvedere Torso*, and the *Laocoön*, while the *Capitoline Venus* was the best-known example of a classical female nude. Renaissance artists studied these and many other classical sculptures, and often included references to them in their work to display their skill and knowledge.

Subjects that gave artists the opportunity to show their skill at painting or sculpting the nude became increasingly popular in the Renaissance. In addition to religious subjects—which accounted

---

Classical figure sculptures had an immense influence on Renaissance painters and sculptors

---

for most of the work ordered from artists—scenes and figures from classical mythology became more and more popular. The use of nudes in paintings and sculptures based on myths was less likely to cause offense than in religious art.

TWO CONTRASTING DAVIDS
Artists also used the human form to express different ideas, something clearly demonstrated by two very different sculptures of the same subject: Donatello's and Michelangelo's statues of the Old Testament hero David. Donatello's *David* (completed around 1440) was the first life-size bronze sculpture of a nude made since Roman times. It portrays David as a graceful, lithe young boy, clad only in boots and a hat, and resting a foot on the head of Goliath, whom he has slain. While Donatello's *David* is elegant, Michelangelo's sculpture (1501–1504) is a solid portrayal of strength. It is a

Below: Leonardo da Vinci's drawing of "Vitruvian man." It shows how the human body—with arms and legs outstretched—fits into both a square and a circle. It was the best known of many Renaissance studies in which artists tried to relate the human form to ideal shapes and formulas.

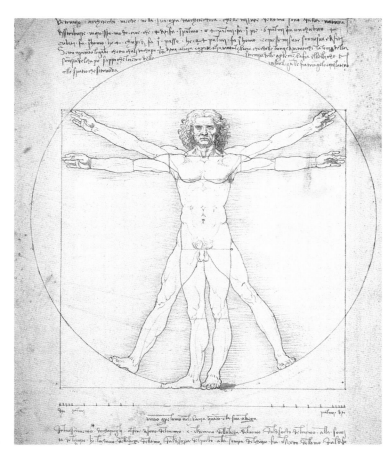

NORTHERN EUROPEAN NUDES

In northern Europe the medieval notion that nudity in art was only acceptable to make a moral point remained in force for longer than in Italy. By the beginning of the 16th century, however, themes and ideas from Italy were beginning to filter through, and German artists like Lucas Cranach (1472–1553) painted scenes from classical mythology with female nudes. However, the approach of northern artists was different from that of the Italians. They did not seek to analyze the structure of the body or to idealize its appearance. They were more concerned with surface detail and real appearances. As a result, many nudes by northern artists do not look as convincing as Italian examples. The German artist Albrecht Dürer (1471–1528) was the first to try to combine the two traditions. He visited Italy on several occasions and was inspired by artists he met there. He became interested in classical notions of proportion and in his engraving *Adam and Eve* (1504) sought to portray the perfect male and female body through careful measurement, as Greek, Roman, and Italian artists had before.

Right: **Venus and Cupid Carrying the Honeycomb** *by Lucas Cranach. Although Cranach responded to the fashion for nudes, his figures, with their elongated limbs, are far from lifelike.*

massive marble statue measuring about 13 ft (4m) high, showing David as a muscular, athletic hero. Such was the youth, vigor, and strength of Michelangelo's portrayal that the rulers of Florence (where the sculpture stood) saw it as symbolizing the power of their republic. Michelangelo produced some of the most famous male nudes of the Renaissance. His figures are powerful and muscular, often in poses suggesting great strength and energy. He was profoundly influenced by classical sculpture, although his work is also highly individual in its intensity and drama.

Something both Michelangelo and Donatello's sculptures of David have in common is the pose known as *contrapposto*, in which most of the body's weight is supported on one leg, while the other is slightly bent at the knee. This stance causes the hips, shoulders, and upper body to be at slight angles and is very difficult to capture. Complex poses with twisting,

In the 16th century the female nude became an important theme in art

turning bodies were very popular in the Renaissance because they displayed the artist's skill. In the work of some artists such as Giambologna (1529–1608) the portrayal of extremely complex poses became an end in itself.

VENUS A POPULAR SUBJECT

In the 16th century the female nude also became an important theme. This was closely related to the increased number of paintings commissioned by wealthy, scholarly men for their private homes and by the increased interest in classical mythology. Venus, goddess of love, was the most popular subject. The Florentine painter Sandro Botticelli (about 1445–1510) painted the first large-scale paintings based on classical mythology in which he also revived the classical ideal of the female nude. In *The Birth of Venus* (about 1485) he shows the goddess as a slender beauty with a dreamy, innocent expression. She modestly covers her body in a pose based on the *Capitoline Venus*.

In the 16th century, however, Venetian artists such as Giorgione (1477–1510) and particularly Titian (about 1487–1576) emphasized the sensual qualities of the female body. They painted Venus with soft, glowing tones, reclining (leaning or lying down), and looking out of the picture with an inviting gaze. The beauty and allure of Titian's nudes like the *Venus of Urbino* (about 1538) and *Danaë* (1554) influenced generations of artists.

Left: Titian's **Venus of Urbino** *(about 1538), one of the most famous pictures of a female nude ever made. It shows the goddess Venus as an alluring lady in her bedroom, looking out of the picture with an inviting gaze.*

PRAEFATIO IOHANNIS ARGIROPYLI BIZĀ
TII IN PHISICORVM ARISTOTELIS LIBROS AD
PRESTANTISSIMVM VIRVM PETRVM MEDI
CEM

OHANNES. ARGI
ROPILVS BIZAN
TIVS. MAGNIFIC
VIRO PETRO. ME

Humanism

In Italy in the 15th century the word *umanistà* or "humanist" meant a teacher of the "humanities" —that is, secular (nonreligious) subjects concerned with understanding people's place in the world. The humanist outlook was based on a renewed interest in ancient Greek and Roman civilization and came to shape

Above: A page from a 15th-century translation of a work by the ancient Greek philosopher Aristotle. Humanist scholars read and translated many classical texts.

the whole spirit of the Renaissance— including its art, architecture, literature, and politics. In the 19th century historians coined the term "humanism" to describe this new spirit, which they believed set the Renaissance apart from the earlier medieval age.

In 1423 a professor at the university of Padua, Vittorino da Feltre (1378– 1446), went to the nearby city of Mantua to set up a new school for its ruler, Gianfrancesco Gonzaga. Da Feltre called the school La Giocosa, or "The House of Joy," and his pupils included not only Gonzaga's sons but also those of other noble families as well as the gifted sons of poorer families. One of his most notable pupils was Federigo da Montefeltro (1422–1482), who later became a famous duke of Urbino.

A NEW TYPE OF EDUCATION
The curriculum at La Giocosa was very different from that of most other schools of the time. Unusually, it centered on teaching the language and literature of ancient Greece and Rome. It also featured math, geometry, music, and rhetoric (the art of speaking eloquently or persuasively), as well as physical education and games. The corporal punishment of pupils was forbidden. The new thinking behind the school was based on the ideas of Pietro Paolo Vergerio (1370–1444/45), who in about 1402 had published an influential treatise on education called *On the Conduct of Honorable Men*.

Vergerio and his followers believed that the role of education was to nurture well-balanced individuals— "all-rounders" who were fit in both body and mind. Such individuals, they thought, were likely to be good citizens as well as good Christians, serving their society as well as God. Many humanist schools like La Giocosa were founded in Italian ducal courts in the 15th century.

HUMANIST IDEAS

The Italian humanists believed that it was the ancient, or "classical," Greeks and Romans who had made the greatest achievements in the humanities, and they looked afresh at their writings in order to find inspiration for their own work. One of the first people to reassess the heritage of the classical world was Petrarch (1304–1374), who is therefore sometimes

> *A new spirit of inquiry, experimentation, and openness characterized the Renaissance*

known as the "father of humanism." In addition to writing poetry, Petrarch collected Latin manuscripts and studied them in depth. He wrote biographies of famous men from classical times as well as dialogues—or imaginary conversations—about philosophy that were modeled on those written by the ancient Greeks and Romans.

Throughout his work Petrarch attacked scholasticism—the system of thought that dominated the medieval world, which rigidly followed the traditional teachings of the church. Like later humanists, Petrarch believed that scholars, writers, thinkers, and politicians alike should try to understand and analyze the world around them, rather than simply accepting established or preconceived ideas. It

was this new spirit of inquiry, experimentation, and openness that characterized the Renaissance.

The humanists saw in the classical world an underlying philosophy, which they believed could help improve their own society. This philosophy was summed up in the Latin concept of *humanitas,* or "humanity." *Humanitas* meant much more than loving kindness, which is the usual meaning of

Below: A 15th-century portrait of the Italian poet and scholar Petrarch. It comes from a series of pictures of famous men made for Federigo da Montefeltro's study in his palace in Urbino.

PETRARCHAE

"humanity" today. It encompassed not only compassion and mercy, but also practical virtues like courage, honor, eloquence, moderation, and judgment.

Someone with *humanitas* was an all-round individual, who tried to reach their full potential as a human being and also to serve their fellow men and women. For the humanists the ideal was therefore someone who was not only learned and thoughtful but also practical and active in public affairs—in short, both a thinker and a "doer." Many of these ideas were summed up by the writer Baldassare Castiglione (1478–1529) in his celebrated treatise the *Book of the Courtier* (1528).

Many individuals took up the humanists' challenge. As duke of Urbino, the adult Federigo da Montefeltro was a scholar and patron of the arts as well as a brilliant soldier and statesman. He assembled a massive collection of books, commissioned works from bold and original artists like Piero della Francesca, and had scholars read out classical books to him during mealtimes. He also conducted a series of a wars in central Italy and used the money he won in his campaigns to rebuild Urbino as an "ideal city."

Leon Battista Alberti (1404–1472) was another outstanding example of the humanist ideal. Alberti was a churchman with a passionate interest in many subjects. He wrote influential books about disciplines as diverse as painting, sculpture, architecture, geography, and the family, and also designed buildings. Because of his wide-ranging interests and talents the 19th-century historian Jakob Burckhardt called Alberti a "universal man." The humanists' belief in human achievement and in human beings' capacity for self-improvement was most famously proclaimed by the writer Giovanni Pico della Mirandola (1463–1494) in his *Oration on the Dignity of Man* (1486).

DEVELOPMENT OF HUMANISM

During the late 15th and early 16th centuries the ideas of the Italian humanists spread throughout Europe. Castiglione's *Book of the Courtier* was especially widely read. At many courts royal children were given a thoroughly humanist education. In England, for example, the young Princess Elizabeth (later Queen Elizabeth I) was taught by the English humanist Roger Ascham (1515–1568), under whom she quickly mastered Latin, Greek, rhetoric, and

Below: **The Brera Altarpiece** *(1470s)* *by Piero della Francesca. The painting shows Federigo da Montefeltro wearing armor and kneeling in prayer to the Virgin and Child, representing Federigo as both a soldier and a pious man.*

philosophy. As queen she was not only a skillful ruler but an enlightened patron of the arts.

In northern Europe the greatest humanist was Desiderius Erasmus (about 1466–1536). Like Petrarch, he fiercely attacked medieval scholasticism and pedantry. He also studied the Bible with the same intelligence and lack of prejudice that the humanists brought to the writings of ancient Greece and Rome. Erasmus's ideas deeply influenced the work of many writers of the northern Renaissance, including the French essayists François Rabelais and Michel de Montaigne.

As humanism spread, it lost much of its original energy and unity of ideas. Even in Italy, where the movement began, thinkers and writers began to emphasize different aspects of humanism to the detriment of others. The humanists continued to find support for their ideas in the classical

---

Humanism had a powerful influence over thought, education, and politics

---

past, but now the beliefs of ancient writers came to seem increasingly diverse and less straightforward.

In Florence, for example, Marsilio Ficino (1433–1499), the head of the Platonic Academy founded by Cosimo de Medici, developed a highly spiritual version of humanism. Ficino's ideas, derived from the writings of the ancient Greek philosopher Plato, proved very influential but had little to do with the practical, "real" world. One Florentine even accused Pico della Mirandola, who was a follower of

Left: A 16th-century sculpture of the Renaissance philosopher Marsilio Ficino. Ficino translated Plato's works into Latin and was head of the Platonic Academy in Florence. He is shown here as a scholar, holding a large book.

Ficino, of abandoning his public duties altogether for a private world of study and contemplation.

Another humanist from Florence, the diplomat and writer Niccolò Machiavelli (1469–1527), went to the other extreme, emphasizing the importance of a hard-headed, realistic attitude to public affairs and to human nature. He used the history of Greece and Rome to show how badly—rather than how well—men and women could behave, and argued that political rule had nothing to do with morality.

Despite such contradictions, Renaissance humanism had a powerful influence over European thought, education, and politics for centuries after. Humanist ideas about human dignity, civic duty, and the importance of an all-round education and an open, questioning mind are all key modern democratic values, even if we have largely forgotten their original source in the classical world.

India

In the 15th and 16th centuries the area that we today know as India was made up of a number of independent states of varying degrees of size and power. The most important of them were the Islamic Mogul Empire, which covered most of northern India by the late 16th century, and the Hindu kingdom of Vijayanagar in the southeast.

In the late Middle Ages northern India was dominated by the Islamic Delhi Sultanate. The first Muslim excursions into the area came in the early 11th century, when the Turkic leader Mahmud of Ghazni (971–1030) made a number of raids into northern India from his base in what is now Afghanistan. At that time northern India was dominated by the Rajputs— warrior Hindu clans. Mahmud defeated the Rajputs, looted Hindu temples, and forcibly converted the inhabitants of the area. Mahmud established a powerful state based in the Punjab region that lasted until the 12th century, when another Muslim leader, Muhammad of Ghur (died 1206), overthrew his dynasty.

By the end of the 13th century Muhammad's successors had managed to create a sizable empire, the capital of which was the city of Delhi. The Delhi Sultanate, as it has come to be known, dominated northern India for 200 years. Although the sultanate was extremely powerful, it was often riven by internal disputes, and there were frequent civil wars and struggles for power between rival factions.

The Delhi Sultanate was already in decline when the great Mongol leader Tamerlane (1336–1405) invaded India in 1398. Tamerlane ruled over a vast empire that stretched over much of Central Asia. In a short campaign Tamerlane swept through northern India before inflicting a decisive defeat on the sultanate at the battle of Panipat. He slaughtered 100,000 captives before marching on Delhi itself. The city was ransacked and much of its population killed. Tamerlane then returned to Central Asia, destroying

Above: This illustration from a Mogul manuscript shows Akbar, the greatest of the Mogul emperors of India, crossing the Ganges River on an elephant during one of his many military campaigns.

everything that lay in his path. After this devastating campaign Delhi never returned to its former greatness.

Delhi was now just one of several states competing for power. Others included Gujarat, Bengal, and Jaunpur. Although there was a slight upturn in

---

After Tamerlane's invasion Delhi never returned to its former greatness

---

the fortunes of the Delhi Sultanate in the second half of the 15th century under the Lodi dynasty, they could not extend their power beyond the Punjab. Northern India remained fragmented until the coming of the Mogul Empire in the early 16th century.

THE MOGUL EMPIRE

By the time of the reign of the Sultan Ibrahim Lodi (ruled 1517–1526) the Delhi Sultanate was having great difficulty controlling its territories. A powerful Central Asian leader named Babur (1483–1530) took advantage of the situation and invaded northern India in 1526. Even though they were heavily outnumbered, Babur's mobile cavalry forces and artillery managed to inflict a heavy defeat on a Lodi army at Panipat in April 1526. He occupied Delhi a few days later. This event marked the beginning of the Mogul (or Mughal) Empire. The name is derived from the Persian word for Mongol.

In the next few years Babur extended the area under his control westward. In 1527 he defeated a huge Hindu Rajput army at the battle of Khanua, despite the fact that his forces were outnumbered by five to one.

MOGUL ART

Art flourished in the Mogul Empire, mainly in the form of remarkably detailed manuscript illustrations and miniature paintings. Traditionally, the religion of Islam banned the depiction of the human form in art, but the emperors encouraged their court painters to ignore this restriction. Mogul paintings usually took episodes from history and folk tales as their subject. They were influenced by the heavily stylized art of Persia, although gradually Mogul art developed a more naturalistic (or lifelike) style of its own.

The emperor Akbar was a particularly enthusiastic patron of the arts and commissioned hundreds of paintings, many of which still survive. Among the most famous are a series of illustrations to the great Hindu epic, the *Mahabharata*. Mogul art continued to develop during the reign of Akbar's son and successor, Jahangir, through the work of artists such as Abu al-Hasan and Bishandas.

Above: This 16th-century Mogul manuscript illustration comes from a book telling the story of Babur.

Further victories meant that by 1529 the Mogul Empire covered most of northern India.

On his death in 1530 Babur was succeeded by his son Humayun (1508–1556). However, Humayun lost control of his empire to rebel forces and was forced to flee to Persia. Although he managed to regain some of his territories, the empire that he left to his 13-year-old son Akbar (1542 –1605) in 1556 was a shadow of the one that had existed 25 years earlier. Fortunately for the Mogul dynasty, Akbar was to prove one of the most capable rulers of his time.

THE REIGN OF AKBAR

Almost immediately Akbar was faced with a military challenge from the powerful Hindu general Hemu, who was based to the south in the Ganges Valley. Helped by his adviser Bairam, Akbar managed to defeat Hemu at Panipat. Over the next four years the young emperor consolidated his grip on northern India. In 1560 Akbar dismissed Bairam and began to rule for himself.

Below: The tomb of the Mogul emperor Humayun in Delhi, a classic example of Mogul architecture. Its domes and arches reflect the Turkic origins of the Moguls.

During the next 40 years of his reign Akbar greatly added to the territories under his control. Soon the Mogul Empire stretched from Gujarat on the west coast to Bengal on the east. Eventually, it reached as far as Kandesh in the south. Despite these great military victories, however, Akbar is remembered as much for the cultural impact of his reign as for his achievements as a soldier.

Previous Muslim rulers had attempted to impose both their culture and their religion on the mainly Hindu population. Akbar realized that such a policy was a recipe for disaster, and that to build a stable empire, he needed to create one that was culturally united. One of the first steps that he took to achieve this goal came in 1562, when he married a Hindu princess. As a Muslim, Akbar was entitled to four wives, and he went on to marry another Hindu, a Muslim, and a Christian. In this way Akbar's family mirrored the empire as a whole in its mixture of religions.

Akbar also tried to promote religious harmony through his

taxation policy. For centuries Islamic rulers had imposed a special tax on Hindus. Akbar abolished it, greatly reducing the general burden of taxation on his subjects. He also passed a law forbidding any form of forced conversion to Islam. Importantly, Hindus were allowed to play a significant role in the administration of the empire, which was divided into 15 provinces, each subdivided into separate districts. By placing locally born people in positions of authority, Akbar was able to reduce resentment against Mogul rule.

During Akbar's reign the arts and culture flourished. A distinctive Mogul style of architecture grew up that blended Persian and traditional Indian elements. The empire became famous for the quality of its textiles and glasswork, while painters and poets also flocked to Akbar's court. Although Persian was the official language of the court, it gradually merged with earlier languages of the area to form Hindi, now the most widespread language of present-day India.

Akbar's reign came to an end in 1605, when he was poisoned by his own son, Jahangir (1569–1627). The Mogul Empire continued to expand under the rule of Jahangir and was to dominate northern India until the middle of the 18th century.

SOUTHERN INDIA

Despite their great power, the Moguls never brought southern India under their control. A number of different southern states jostled for power during the 15th and 16th centuries, but the most successful was undoubtedly the Hindu Vijayanagar Empire. It was founded in 1336 and quickly expanded until it stretched from coast to coast. Vijayanagar prospered economically

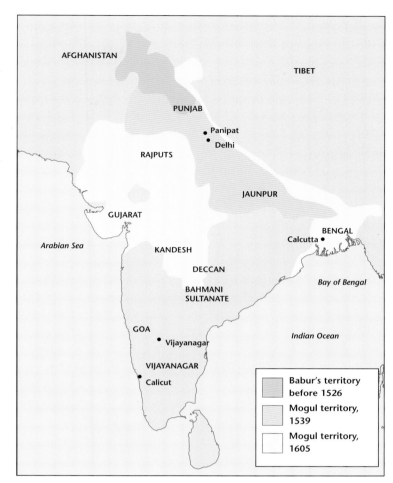

Above: This map shows the expansion of Mogul territory from the area ruled by Babur before his invasion of northern India in 1526 to the extent of the Mogul Empire at the death of Akbar in 1605.

from maritime trade with Europe and reached the height of its power under Krishna Deva Raya (ruled 1509–1527) in the early 16th century. At the heart of the empire lay the magnificent city of Vijayanagar itself, the site of imposing temples and palaces.

Throughout its history Vijayanagar fought wars against the Muslim states that lay to its north, most notably the Bahmani Sultanate that was based in the Deccan. For centuries Vijayanagar successfully managed to protect its territory, but in 1565 an alliance of five Muslim kingdoms inflicted a crushing defeat on the empire at the battle of Talikota. The city of Vijayanagar itself was destroyed shortly afterward, and the empire disintegrated into a number of small states.

INDIAN SOCIETY

Mogul India was a place of great contrast between rich and poor. The rich enjoyed lives of enormous luxury, and the courts of emperors such as Babur and Akbar were the scenes of lavish celebrations as noblemen tried to outdo each other in displays of wealth. In many regional towns merchants grew rich through the export of spices, while tax collectors abused their positions to increase their own wealth.

However, the vast majority of people who lived in the Mogul Empire were poor farmers. Their homes were simple rush or mud huts with thatched roofs, and they existed on a diet of rice and corn. Bad harvests were a frequent problem and could lead to great famines. Another constant threat was disease—like Europe, India was often afflicted by plague.

The poor were restricted in their social movement by the caste system, which tied people to a particular profession from the day they were born. Members of different castes could not marry one another and had to follow special instructions as to what they could eat. Although the caste system was mainly associated with the Hindu religion, it continued to thrive under the rule of the Muslim Moguls.

Right: This 16th-century manuscript illustration shows a wedding celebration. In Mogul India the rich lived extremely lavish lifestyles.

THE PORTUGUESE IN INDIA

Europeans had traded with India for centuries, but it was not until 1498 that a western explorer managed to discover a sea route to the continent. In that year a small number of Portuguese ships under the command of Vasco da Gama (about 1460–1524) sailed around the Cape of Good Hope (the southern tip of Africa). They continued north up the east coast of Africa, finally crossing the Indian ocean to reach Calicut.

A great deal of money could be made from importing spices from the east, and soon other Portuguese sailors arrived to establish permanent trading posts. Among the most important was Afonso de Albuquerque (1453–1515). Within 15 years he had taken control of a long strip of the western coast of India, sometimes through force, though often with the blessing of nearby rulers who could benefit from trade with Europe. The powerful state of Gujarat to the north made several military attempts to dislodge the newcomers, but these attacks had little success. Goa, the area controlled by the Portuguese, reached the height of its wealth and power in the late 16th century, when it lay at the heart of a huge trading empire.

SEE ALSO

♦ Exploration
♦ Islam
♦ Navigation
♦ Portugal
♦ Trade

Inquisition

Left: This painting shows the astronomer Galileo Galilei being interrogated by the Inquisition in Rome in 1633. Threatened with torture, he renounced his heretical belief that the earth moves around the sun and was sentenced to house arrest. A heretic who refused to recant could be burned at the stake.

Throughout the history of the Catholic church there have always been Christians who have chosen to hold religious ideas different from those of the majority of believers. These people or groups are known as heretics (from the Greek for "to choose"). In the Middle Ages heretics were seen as a danger because it was thought their ideas might damage and divide the church. So in 1231, in response to this problem, Pope Gregory IX set up an organization called the Inquisition in Rome. Its task was to seek out heretics and force them to give up their beliefs.

The Inquisition followed a set method. Inquisitors—usually friars from the Franciscan or Dominican orders—were sent out to a particular region, most often in southern France and northern Italy. On arrival they would allow about a month for anyone practicing a heresy to give themselves up. Those who did so within this period were given a relatively mild punishment, such as being made to go on a fast or a pilgrimage. After the deadline passed, however, those believed to be heretics were brought to trial. If found guilty, they could be imprisoned, have their property taken away, or be handed over to the civic authorities to be burned at the stake. Before their trial accused heretics were often kept in jail, and some were tortured to encourage them to confess.

THE INQUISITION SPREADS

In 1478 a second form of the Inquisition was set up in Spain. It soon came under the leadership of a friar named Tomas de Torquemada

THE USE OF TORTURE

In medieval and Renaissance times governments routinely used torture. The church authorized its use in 1252, when Pope Innocent IV decreed that it was permissible for Inquisitors to inflict it on suspected heretics to get them to confess. The use of torture became especially widespread in the early days of the Spanish Inquisition.

Methods of torture varied from one region to another, but in most countries simple instruments such as whips and iron claws were used to rip the flesh of the victim. One popular device was the rack, where the victim was laid across a board with his hands and feet tied to ropes. These ropes were then slowly wound around rollers, stretching the body until the joints were dislocated. Other devices included a hanging technique called the strappado and a neck clamp dubbed the heretic's fork. Thumbscrews were used in conjunction with these devices to increase the pain. In the face of such treatment it is unsurprising that most suspected heretics confessed to their sins and adopted official church teachings.

Above: An illustration showing German inquisitors obtaining confessions. One victim is on the rack, and another is strung up by his wrists on the strappado.

SEE ALSO

♦ Catholic
  Church
♦ Counter
  Reformation
♦ Crime and
  Punishment
♦ Papacy
♦ Philip II
♦ Spain

(1420–1498), when it gained a widespread reputation for ferocity and the use of torture. Under Torquemada an estimated 2,000 victims were burned to death. The Spanish Inquisition was mainly aimed at Spanish Jews and Muslims who had become Christians in order to avoid persecution but who were believed to be practicing their old religion in secret. Later, Protestants were also targeted. Tribunals were set up all around Spain, as well as in the Spanish colonies of Mexico and Peru, where local healers were accused of sorcery. The accused were sentenced at an auto-da-fé ("act of faith"), a public declaration of the sentence, which was usually death by burning.

A third form of the Inquisition was established in 1542 in Rome to target Protestants in Italy. However, it also attacked Catholic thinkers whose ideas were in conflict with the church. Well-known victims included the philosopher Tommaso Campanella, who

The Spanish Inquisition gained a widespread reputation for ferocity

was imprisoned, the astronomer Galileo Galilei, who was put under house arrest, and the philosopher Giordano Bruno, who was burned at the stake. The Roman Inquisition was generally less severe than its Spanish counterpart, although it was very active in the mid-16th century, when it gained a reputation for brutality.

Islam

Islam, one of the world's great religions, was founded by the prophet Muhammad (about 570–632) in the seventh century A.D. By the 14th century Islam had spread to regions far beyond its original home in Arabia. It was the dominant religion throughout the Middle East and in Central Asia, North Africa, western India, and parts of Europe.

The core beliefs of Islam have remained largely unchanged since the time of Muhammad, although many sects (or groups) have since interpreted these beliefs in different ways. Like Christianity and Judaism, Islam is a

---

Muslims believe that human beings must submit to the will of Allah

---

monotheistic religion, which means that its followers, who are called Muslims, believe there is only one god.

Muslims refer to their god as Allah, which is the Arabic word for "God." At the heart of Islam is the belief that human beings must submit to the will of Allah. The word "Islam" itself means "submission." The Islamic holy book is called the Koran (or Qu'ran) and contains the teachings of Allah as revealed to Muhammad. According to Islamic belief, Muhammad was the last and the greatest of many prophets to whom God revealed his will.

After Muhammad's death Islam spread rapidly as Arab armies conquered large areas of North Africa, the eastern Mediterranean, and Central Asia. The Islamic lands were ruled over by a caliph, who was seen as the successor to Muhammad. In 680, however, there was a dispute over who should become the next caliph, and Muslims divided into two groups. The dominant group, the Sunnis, believed that any man could be a caliph as long as he was a devout Muslim. The Shi'ites, by contrast, believed that Muhammad had appointed his son-in-law, Ali, as his successor and that only Ali's descendants were entitled to rule. Although the Sunnis were the more powerful force in the Islamic world, the differences between the two groups deepened over the centuries, frequently causing war and conflict.

The empire ruled by the caliph, called the caliphate, became so large that by the ninth century regional rulers known as emirs had emerged. In the following centuries migrating peoples such as the Turks and Mongols converted to Islam, and founded their own powerful dynasties of rulers. Their rule rivaled or even replaced traditional centers of Islamic power such as

Above: This copy of the Koran was produced in the early 16th century. The Koran is the holy book of Islam—Muslims believe it contains the word of Allah, as revealed to the prophet Muhammad.

Below: This illustration from a 15th-century religious text shows pilgrims to Mecca worshiping at the Black Stone of the Kaaba, Islam's holiest shrine. Muslims always turn toward the Kaaba when they pray.

Baghdad. By the time of the Renaissance there were three major Muslim empires—the Ottoman Empire, based in present-day Turkey; the Safavid Empire, centered on present-day Iran and Iraq; and the Mogul Empire, which lay to the east in northern India.

THE OTTOMANS

Originally a nomadic Turkic tribe, the Ottomans began their rise to power in the early 14th-century, when they occupied a small region in the north of Anatolia in present-day Turkey. Gradually, the warlike Ottomans

Below: This illustration from a 15th-century religious text shows pilgrims to Mecca worshiping at the Black Stone of the Kaaba, Islam's holiest shrine. Muslims always turn toward the Kaaba when they pray.

expanded their territory, largely at the expense of the neighboring Christian Byzantine Empire. The Byzantine capital Constantinople eventually fell in 1453, by which time the Ottomans controlled Greece and much of the Balkans. The empire continued to expand in the 16th century. In 1517 the Ottoman sultan Selim I (ruled 1512–1520) defeated a rival Muslim state, that of the Mamluks, and so gained control of Egypt, Syria, and Palestine. The Ottoman Turks reached the height of their power under the reign of Selim's son, Suleyman the Magnificent (ruled 1520–1566), when they dominated the whole of the eastern Mediterranean.

To the east of the Ottoman lands lay the Safavid Empire. The Safavids were Shi'ite Muslims and were often engaged in war against their Sunni neighbors the Ottomans. The dynasty was founded by Ismail I in the early 16th century, and by 1514 the Safavids controlled most of present-day Iran and much of Iraq. In August of that year, however, Ismail was defeated in battle by his Ottoman rival Selim I, and Safavid power declined until the reign of Abbas I (1588–1629). Abbas eventually regained lands taken by the Ottomans and created a wealthy, stable, and extremely powerful Shi'ite state.

THE MOGUL EMPIRE

The third great Muslim empire of the 15th and 16th centuries was the Mogul Empire of India. It was founded in the early 16th century by a Central Asian leader called Babur. Under his successors Humayun and Akbar it grew to cover a huge area of northern India. The Mogul Empire differed from its Ottoman and Safavid counterparts in the fact that the majority of its inhabitants were not Muslims but

Hindus. However, by pursuing a policy of religious tolerance, the empire's Muslim rulers managed to keep it relatively stable and united. Other smaller Muslim states that thrived in the Renaissance period included Aceh, based on the island of Sumatra in present-day Indonesia, and the Songhai Empire of West Africa.

ISLAMIC CULTURE

Islamic culture grew out of the ancient, pre-Islamic traditions of Arabia and other countries. However, early Islamic thinkers also eagerly studied the writings of other cultures, especially ancient Greece and Rome. Muslim scholars translated Greek and Roman works into Arabic and so preserved many ancient texts that might otherwise have been lost to western Europe. Muslims also developed their own traditions in every area of learning, including math, medicine, philosophy, and politics, binding them closely to the teachings of their religion. Although the Christian and Islamic worlds were often in conflict in

both medieval and Renaissance times, there was also much trade and cultural contact between the two regions. Islamic scholarship had a great impact

THE FIVE PILLARS

There are five fundamental obligations in Islam, called the Five Pillars. They lay down the beliefs and duties of both the individual and the community as a whole. The first pillar is the profession of faith in Allah: "There is no god but Allah; Muhammad is the prophet of Allah." Every Muslim has to make this profession at least once in his or her lifetime. The second pillar is prayer. Every Muslim must pray at five set times every day, although exceptions are made for the sick, dying, or those on a journey. Muslims may pray alone or together at a religious building called a mosque.

The third pillar is a religious tax known as *zakat*. Today *zakat* is usually paid voluntarily, but in earlier times all Muslims had to pay between 5 and 10 percent of their goods or earnings to the local religious authorities. The fourth pillar is fasting during the Muslim month of Ramadan. During Ramadan Muslims must not eat or drink from dawn until dusk. The fifth pillar is the pilgrimage to Mecca—the birthplace of Muhammad and the most holy place in Islam. Every Muslim must undertake the pilgrimage, or *hajj*, once in a lifetime if he or she is physically able and can afford to do so.

on that of western Europe. Perhaps the most important contribution the Islamic world made was that of Arabic numerals, which replaced the more cumbersome Roman numeral system in Europe.

ART AND ARCHITECTURE

Architecture was another art that was highly developed in the Islamic world, where the most important buildings were mosques. They were usually beautifully decorated with marble, mosaics, and intricately carved wood-work. From early on Islamic law prohibited paintings or sculptures of living things in mosques, although there is no such rule in the Koran. Decoration was confined to rich, abstract patterns and the flowing scripts used by the Persians and Arabians. Outside of the mosques, however, artists—including book illustrators, potters, and painters— often did depict humans, animals, and plants in their work, and many beautiful examples of their craft survive today. The art of working with textiles also thrived in Islamic countries, and the brilliantly patterned carpets produced in these regions were much admired in Renaissance Europe.

Right: This 16th-century carpet was made in the city of Kashan in Persia (present-day Iran). It is decorated with pictures of animals. Famous for their beauty, Persian carpets were highly valued in western Europe.

SEE ALSO

♦ Africa
♦ India
♦ Ottoman Empire
♦ Spain
♦ Textiles

Italy

During the Renaissance Italy was not the unified country that it is today. From the collapse of the Roman Empire in the fifth century A.D. until 1870, when the country was finally unified, the Italian peninsula was a complex patchwork of kingdoms, duchies, republics, and other lands. Repeated foreign invasions added to the country's disarray.

The diverse landscapes and cultures that lay within Italy encouraged disunity. The fertile north, with its mild climate, contrasted with the dry, sun-baked south. There were many different dialects of Italian, and people from different parts of the country often could not understand one another. The mountainous terrain also meant that travel between towns and cities was difficult, and many places were very isolated. Few people thought of "Italy" as a unified country. Their loyalty and patriotism were for their local town or city or, at most, for their region. There was often a fierce rivalry between neighbors, which sometimes broke out into war.

On the eve of the Renaissance the Italian peninsula was more divided than ever. In the south of the country were two large kingdoms: Naples and Sicily. Both were ruled by foreign powers—Sicily by a royal family from the Spanish kingdom of Aragon and Naples by a French noble family called the Angevins. The kingdoms were frequently at war with each other, and both were poor and backward.

To the north of the kingdom of Naples were the Papal States. They

> ## The land in the center and north of Italy was much more prosperous than the south

included not only Rome and its surrounding lands but also regions far to the northeast. The popes had ruled over lands in central Italy since the eighth century. For much of the 14th century, however, unrest among the local lords forced the popes to abandon Italy and take up residence in southern France, at Avignon. In many areas the lords took the opportunity to seize power. Even after the popes returned to Rome in 1377, they continued to find it difficult to assert their power over their lands for many decades.

The land in the center and north of Italy was much more prosperous than the south. During the Middle Ages many of its numerous towns and cities had grown rich through trade and manufacture. Gradually, they were able to assert their independence from their traditional rulers, the pope and the Holy Roman emperor, and establish themselves as independent communes, or city-states.

At first the communes were governed by councils elected by assemblies of leading citizens. By the 14th century, however, many of the communes had fallen into the hands of a single ruler, called a *signore*, who often passed his power on to his son. This kind of one-man rule was called a *signoria*. Many

Right: This 15th-century painting shows the fleet of the Spanish king Ferdinand of Aragon (1452–1516) in Naples harbor. The Spanish took control of Naples from the French Angevins in 1422. The imposing fortress is the Castel Nuovo, or "new castle," which was built by the Angevins in 1282.

other communes held on to the old way of doing things and proclaimed themselves republics. Even in these former communes, however, power tended to gather in the hands of a few leading families.

THREE GREAT STATES

In the late 14th century three states dominated the affairs of central and northern Italy: Milan, Venice, and Florence. Each had gradually trans-

> *Three states dominated the affairs of central and northern Italy: Milan, Venice, and Florence*

formed itself from a small state based around a single city into a large "territorial" state that encompassed surrounding lands and cities.

Milan, in the northwest, was a *signoria* ruled by the wealthy Visconti family. By a mixture of war and negotiation the ambitious Visconti conquered territory far to the south and west. To the east of Milan, on the coast of the Adriatic Sea, was the republic of Venice. The city, built on a group of islands in a lagoon, was a flourishing port. The Republic of Florence, to the south of Milan, was an important center for banking and manufacture. There were many other smaller republics and *signorie*, but the fate of all of them was largely tied up with the affairs of the greater powers that surrounded them.

It was from the wealthy, competitive cities of northern and central Italy that the cultural flowering that we today call the Renaissance first emerged. In

particular, the city governments of republics such as Florence, Venice, and Siena were important patrons of artists, writers, and humanist scholars, and funded splendid new buildings that proclaimed their city's greatness. The less prosperous and politically weaker cities of Rome and Naples became important centers of Renaissance culture only later.

WAR, PEACE, AND DIPLOMACY

The first half of the 15th century was dominated by war, as the various states competed with one another for political and economic power. In the south the Aragonese and Angevins struggled for control of the Kingdom of Naples, while in the north the two great republics of Venice and Florence allied themselves against Milan.

By contrast, the second half of the 15th century was a time of relative

Above: A map showing the different states and principal cities in Italy around 1500. The balance of power in Italy was precarious throughout the Renaissance, as Spain and France fought for domination.

peace. All of the states were tired of war, which wasted their economies. Venice was more concerned about the growing power of the Ottoman Turks than with Italian affairs. In Florence the powerful Medici family, which had dominated the city since 1434, focused on keeping control of the restless cities that lay within its territory.

In 1454 Milan, Florence, Venice, Naples, and the Papal States formed an "Italian league" in which they agreed to fight together against their common enemies. The Peace of Lodi, as the treaty was known, ushered in a new age of diplomacy. Instead of engaging in almost constant warfare, the Italian states tried to settle their differences by

---

Instead of almost constant warfare, the Italian states tried to settle their differences by negotiation

---

negotiation, carried out by skilled ambassadors. The popes were still very weak as political leaders, but they played an important role as diplomats. The Holy See (the Papal court) in Rome became the center of not only Italian but also European diplomacy.

Despite the appearance of unity, the states continued to mistrust one another. Especially feared was Venice, which continued to extend its territories across the mainland. The city's huge navy, flourishing overseas trade, its numerous factories making silks, cotton, and glassware, and stable government made it the envy of all of Europe. Deep down the Italian peninsula was just as divided as it had ever been.

THE ITALIAN WARS

In 1494 the French king Charles VIII (ruled 1483–1498) led his army into northern Italy, swept down the peninsula, and occupied Naples. The French invasion marked the beginning of almost four decades of war and instability in Italy, as the two great rival powers of Europe—France and Spain—struggled to gain supremacy there. Battle after battle wasted the countryside and disrupted trade and industry. The Italian states were power-

WARFARE IN ITALY

For much of the 14th and early 15th centuries Italy was in a state of almost constant warfare as rival cities fought one another. Rather than depending on armies made up of their own citizens, the city-states often hired large, independent armies to fight in the wars. The armies were led by captains known as condottieri, or "contractors." The condottieri often had no loyalty to a particular city or lord, and it was not unusual for them to change sides. The most brilliant of the condottieri sometimes ended up seizing power for themselves. The battles fought in Renaissance Italy were famous for their lack of bloodshed. This was partly due to the fact that they were fought between armies of well-equipped knights, whose heavy armor helped prevent serious injuries. However, probably more important was the attitude of the condottieri. The mercenary commanders' only real incentive was economic, so they were reluctant to risk losing too many of their troops because the soldiers were their only way of making money.

Above: Francesco Sforza (1401–1466) and his condottieri. Sforza was one of the leading condottieri of the Renaissance.

Left: A 16th-century painting showing the entry of the French king Charles VIII into Florence. Charles took the city in 1494 on his way to seize Naples from the Spanish. His invasion forced the temporary expulsion of the Medici family from Florence.

less. Unable to unite against the invaders, they were reduced to joining one side and then the other. Governments and dynasties fell. In Florence, for example, the disillusioned citizens forced the ruling Medici family to flee the city. The rule of the Sforzas in Milan collapsed in 1499.

During the 1520s the Spanish king and Holy Roman emperor Charles V (ruled 1519–1556) fought to bring Italy under his control. The Spanish empire had already absorbed Naples and Sicily in 1503. In 1525 he roundly defeated the French king Francis I (reigned 1515–1547) at the battle of Pavia. In 1527 he sacked Rome, and in 1530 he conquered Florence, where he restored the Medici to power. He also took Milan for Spain. Finally, in 1530 the pope crowned Charles as Holy Roman emperor in Bologna.

THE NEW ITALY

Charles V established a measure of peace and order in Italy that lasted throughout the 16th century and beyond. He allowed Venice, Genoa, and Lucca to continue as republics, and turned many of the old *signorie*, such as Mantua and Parma, into duchies. He left the popes to rule the Papal States. The economy, too, quickly recovered. The population grew, so that by 1600 Italy was the most densely populated land in Europe. Waterlogged countryside was drained and planted to feed the growing population. In the south numerous new towns were built.

Under the new order Rome in particular flourished. The popes transformed the old crumbling city into a magnificent new one. They built splendid churches and laid out broad piazzas, commissioning works from the greatest artists, sculptors, and architects of the day. The art and ideas of the Italian Renaissance spread across Europe, often as kings and armies returned from the wars. At courts everywhere people dressed and even ate in an Italian style. Princes were educated according to Italian humanist ideas. Politically and economically Italy may have been overtaken by other European powers, such as Spain, France, and England. Culturally, however, it still reigned supreme.

Japan

The country of Japan is made up of a group of islands that lie to the east of Russia, China, and Korea. The four main islands are Hokkaido, Honshu, Shikoku, and Kyushu. During the period when the Renaissance was happening in Europe, Japan was ruled by a succession of mighty warlords called shoguns. These generals, the heads of powerful families, ruled in the name of the emperor, who was Japan's spiritual leader. Despite these twin authorities, however, the country was constantly plagued by power struggles between rival factions.

The rule of the shoguns, or shogunate, began in the late 12th century and continued for nearly 700 years, until the late 19th century. For much of the 12th century Japan had been a divided country, a network of great estates, each ruled by a clan leader called a daimyo, with an army of warriors to back him. By the 1190s, however, one family, the Minamoto, had come to dominate the rest. In 1192 the Minamoto chief Minamoto Yoritomo had himself named shogun, or "supreme general," by the emperor. The title was passed down within the Minamoto family for nearly 150 years.

Above: This ink and watercolor landscape is by Sesshu Toyo, one of the greatest artists of the Muromachi period (1338–1573). Sesshu was a Buddhist monk and learned to draw at a Zen temple.

Above: A map of Japan, showing the four main islands —Hokkaido, Honshu, Shikoku, and Kyushu.

century. The shogun's authority disintegrated as rival clans plotted and warred against each other. Despite all the fighting, Japanese arts, including painting, drawing, drama, and architecture, thrived during this time. In the late 16th century Japan was reunited under a series of brilliant shoguns. In 1603 the powerful Tokugawa family took control and ruled Japan for the next 250 years, a period of order and great economic prosperity.

RELATIONS WITH THE WEST
News of Japan first reached Europe by way of the Venetian traveler Marco Polo. Visiting the court of the Chinese emperor Kublai Khan in the late 13th century, Polo heard of a rich land to the east. It was known to the Chinese as Zipangu, which meant "land where the sun rises." In the centuries that followed, many European explorers tried to find Japan, lured on by the hope of gold and spices.

In 1338 a rival clan chief, Ashikaga Takauji, succeeded in defeating the Minamoto and becoming shogun. The Ashikaga family held the title until the 1570s. However, the second half of their rule was marked by fighting and unrest. In 1467 full-scale civil war broke out and continued for over a

The first Europeans to set foot in Japan were the Portuguese, who arrived in the early 1540s. The Spanish missionary Francis Xavier landed in Japan in 1549 and soon began to convert the local people to Christianity.

ARTS UNDER THE ASHIKAGAS

The period in which the Ashikaga clan held power was known as the Muromachi period after the district in the imperial city of Kyoto where the Ashikagas held court. It was a golden age for Japanese arts and crafts, including painting, drawing, calligraphy (the art of writing), and theater. Noh plays were a form of drama that developed in the 14th century. The action of the plays unfolded slowly, accompanied by music, chanting, and dancing.

All forms of art in Japan were influenced by Zen Buddhism, which stressed the notion of *wabi*, or simplicity. In the field of landscape painting, for example, the artist Sesshu Toyo (1420–1506) developed a new, simple, but expressive drawing style. Architects built elegant palaces and temples with sweeping roofs and simple lines, such as the Kinkaku-ji (Golden Temple) in Kyoto, completed in 1397. Beautiful gardens were designed and laid out to encourage peaceful meditation. They featured specially shaped rocks set in beds of gravel raked into rippling patterns. Renewed every day, these areas were supposed to represent mountains and water.

SAMURAI KNIGHTS

The samurai were a class of warriors employed by the rival clans to fight their wars. Samurai weapons included bows and arrows, spears, and particularly long swords called katana, which only the samurai could carry. Warriors rode into battle wearing steel helmets with slitted visors and body armor made of leather strips bound with silken thread. A samurai in full armor was a terrifying sight.

During medieval times the samurai developed a code of conduct known as bushido, which means "the way of the warrior." The code was strongly influenced by the principles of Zen Buddhism. Zen was a branch of the Buddhist religion that emphasized stern discipline and meditation. Samurai knights prized honor above everything else, even life itself. To avoid dishonor such as defeat in battle, a warrior would commit suicide by a method known as hara-kiri, which involved slitting his own belly open with a dagger. Another knight would complete the ritual by beheading his fellow soldier with a sword.

Right: This 18th-century woodblock shows a samurai warrior wielding a katana. The samurai played an important role in Japanese politics until the 19th century.

SEE ALSO

♦ Exploration
♦ Jesuits
♦ Missionaries
♦ Portugal
♦ Trade

He was followed by Portuguese missionaries and then by Portuguese traders, who established a base at Nagasaki. During the late 16th century successive shoguns welcomed European missionaries and traders. The warlords prized the westerners' superior weapons, and thanks to the tireless efforts of the missionaries, many thousands of peasants were converted to Christianity.

The triumph of the Tokugawa clan in 1603 brought an abrupt change in relations with the West, however. The new shogun, Tokugawa Ieyasu, feared invasion by European armies. He ordered all foreigners to leave Japan, forbade his own subjects from traveling abroad, and persecuted Japanese Christians. Virtually all contact with the West was severed, and Japan remained isolated for the next 250 years.

Jesuits

The Jesuits were members of the Society of Jesus, a Roman Catholic religious order of men. The order was founded by the Spanish soldier and nobleman Ignatius of Loyola (1491–1556), who decided to devote himself to a spiritual life while recovering from battle wounds. Ignatius spent many years dedicating himself to prayer, during which time he composed the Spiritual Exercises, a set of instructions, warnings, and suggested meditations designed to bring their reader closer to God.

While attending the University of Paris, Ignatius built up a group of followers who joined him in a vow of poverty and chastity. In 1540 they traveled to Rome, where Pope Paul III formally approved the order as the Society of Jesus, although they soon became known simply as Jesuits.

Above: Saint Ignatius of Loyola, the founder of the Jesuit order.

BECOMING A JESUIT

Before accepting a new member, the Society of Jesus considered a wide variety of issues, including the candidate's age and health, his character and reputation, his motivation and education, and his family's financial situation. An attractive physical appearance was also considered important. There was a long and challenging period of probation. In addition to many years of study (especially of Latin and theology) novice Jesuits underwent intense spiritual training, which usually involved completing the Spiritual Exercises developed by Ignatius, a process that took 30 days. Only men were allowed to train to become Jesuits. However, one woman obtained special permission to join the order—Princess Juana, the daughter of Holy Roman emperor Charles V.

The Jesuit order grew extremely rapidly. It was organized around a very strict hierarchy. The head of the order was the "superior general," who lived in Rome and held the position for life. Originally, the title was held by Ignatius himself. As the title "general" indicates, the Jesuits were organized on almost military lines—they were often seen as soldiers in the fight to defend and preserve Catholicism.

In keeping with the military thinking behind the order, the Jesuits placed a great value on the virtues of discipline and obedience. Each Jesuit was supposed to follow the superior general's instructions precisely. Jesuits also took a special vow of obedience to the pope, which made secular (non-religious) rulers suspicious of them.

The Jesuits' main purpose was to promote and defend the Catholic faith.

Right: A 17th-century painting showing Saint Francis Xavier miraculously calming the sea during his voyage to Japan. The Jesuit missionary introduced Christianity to the country in the mid-16th century.

One way that they did so was through education, a policy that made them very influential in Europe. Within 100 years of its founding the society had established over 500 colleges. A large proportion of the pupils at Jesuit schools came from poor families and paid no fees. They were made to read classical texts and also taught about the sciences—the Jesuits were open-minded about new scientific theories.

MISSIONARY WORK

As European explorers began to discover new lands, Jesuits set out to convert their inhabitants to the Catholic faith. Shortly after the order was founded, Ignatius sent his most trusted follower, Francis Xavier, to preach in Asia. By 1570 there were Jesuits preaching in India, Japan, Brazil, Mexico, and China.

Jesuit missionaries displayed much courage, as well as an ability to adapt to new challenges. Typically, they would focus on converting a country's wealthy and influential elite, in the hope that they in turn would help convert the rest of the population.

The Jesuits were also extremely active in Europe itself. In the 16th century the Catholic church faced a serious challenge from the Protestant Reformation, the movement inspired by Martin Luther that challenged the pope's authority and many core Catholic beliefs. The Jesuits worked tirelessly in northern Europe to prevent the spread of Protestantism and win back areas to the Catholic faith. Their efforts formed a major part of a movement known as the Counter Reformation, which breathed new life into the Catholic church.

Jews and Judaism

During the Renaissance period Jewish people living in Europe faced an enormous amount of hostility. Attacked by both Protestant religious figures in northern Europe and their Catholic equivalents in the south, Jews often found themselves having to flee their homes and move to new lands. However, despite the prejudice that they faced, Jewish merchants and craftsmen had a considerable economic and cultural influence on Renaissance Europe.

Ever since the early Middle Ages Jews had enjoyed a special economic position. Under church law Christians were not allowed to practice usury—lending money to earn interest. The result was that the Jews filled the unpopular, but economically vital, role of moneylenders. From the eighth century onward Jewish merchants also acted as a crucial link between the Christian and Islamic worlds, importing luxury items such as perfumes and spices into Europe and exporting furs and timber.

The wealth that Jewish bankers and merchants built up aroused much resentment. Many Christians also hated Jews for religious reasons. For example, Jews were collectively blamed for crucifying Christ. Anti-Semitism (anti-Jewish feeling) increased from the 11th century onward, thanks partly to discriminatory laws passed by the church. Sometimes Jews became the victims of angry Christian mobs, who needed someone to blame for their economic and other misfortunes.

Left: This illustration from a Jewish religious text shows a rabbi reading from the Torah in a Spanish synagogue. The illustration dates from the 14th century, when Jews played an important role in the government of Spain.

The persecution of Jews in western Europe during the Middle Ages forced many of them to flee to Spain, which was under Muslim control. Muslim states were far more tolerant of other religions than Christian ones, and the

JUDAISM

Judaism is the religion of the ancient Hebrews, who lived in the region that is now Israel, and their descendants, the Jews. It is the oldest of the three great monotheistic religions, the other two being Christianity and Islam (monotheistic religions are those that are based on the worship of a single god).

Judaism was founded by the prophet Abraham, with whom God made a covenant. Its basic beliefs and teachings are contained in a book known as the Torah or Pentateuch, which consists of the first five books of the Old Testament of the Christian Bible. The Torah was revealed by God to the prophet Moses. It contains hundreds of commandments covering every area of daily life from civil law to personal hygiene.

Jews thrived in Spain. However, by the 14th century the Muslims had been driven southward, and the country's new Catholic rulers introduced an aggressive policy of religious unification. Toward the end of the century this led to the conversion of several hundred thousand Jews after a wave of massacres swept through the country.

Many "conversos," or New Christians, were regarded with suspicion, since they continued to live within Jewish communities. They were often thought to practice their old religion secretly. Despite such prejudice, many conversos rose to hold important government posts, a situation that led to further resentment against them. In

THE GHETTO

Ever since Roman times Jews had often lived separately from their Christian and Muslim neighbors. Originally they did so voluntarily as a way of preserving their cultural identity. However, as anti-Semitism grew worse, Jews were increasingly forced to live in segregated areas. Often they were surrounded by walls, the gates of which were locked at night.

These segregated areas came to be known as ghettos. The word came from the Venetian word *gèto*, meaning "foundry," after the Venetians made the Jewish inhabitants of their city live on an island that had formerly been used for ironworking. The Venetian ghetto was established in 1516. It was only one of many official ghettos that were created in the 16th century as the religious upheavals caused by the Protestant Reformation led to an increase in prejudice against Jews. By 1600 there were major Jewish ghettos in Prague, Frankfurt, Trieste, and Rome.

Above: The Jewish ghetto in Venice, established in the early 16th century. The ghetto was extremely crowded, and its inhabitants were forced to live in cramped apartment blocks such as this.

Left: A detail from an illustration in a 15th-century political pamphlet showing Jewish scholars being suckled by "the devil's pig." During this period Jews faced an enormous amount of prejudice and were often seen as being in league with the devil.

1478 the Spanish monarchy responded to this feeling by setting up the Inquisition, an institution that sought out and persecuted people whose religious beliefs differed from those of the Catholic church. Over 20 years several thousand conversos were burned to death for heresy.

EXPULSION FROM SPAIN

In 1492 Spain's remaining Spanish Jews were given the choice of expulsion or conversion. Roughly 60,000 Jews chose to flee to Portugal (from where they were expelled five years later), Holland, Italy, and the Ottoman Empire, whose main city, Constantinople, gained a large Jewish population by 1600.

Wherever they settled, Jewish exiles had a significant effect on the economies of their host countries. In Holland, for example, their wealth, experience, and wide-ranging contacts contributed to Amsterdam's rise as the world's principal money market. In Constantinople Jewish craftsmen were actively welcomed by the Ottoman Sultan Mehmed II as part of his drive to restore the city to its former glories.

In the early 16th century both the Protestant Reformation and the Catholic Counter Reformation that followed it led to further persecution of Jews. When German Jews showed no sign of converting to Protestantism, Martin Luther adopted a very aggressive stance, demanding that synagogues should be burned to the ground. Jews also faced hostility in southern European countries, as a revival of Catholicism led to attacks on all other religious groups. In 1555 Pope Paul IV ordered that Jews who lived in the Papal States should be forced to live in a walled section of their city.

Increased religious persecution in western Europe caused many Jews to move eastward. Many settled in Poland, where the number of Jews rose from 50,000 in 1500 to 500,000 in 1650. There the Jews flourished, forming a class of traders and bankers who greatly contributed to the wealth of the country. The Jews even formed their own government, known as the Council of the Four Lands, which operated independently of the Polish state and wielded considerable power.

SEE ALSO

♦ Constantinople
♦ Eastern Europe
♦ Inquisition
♦ Spain

Joan of Arc

A French national heroine, Joan of Arc (about 1412–1431) helped turn the tide of the Hundred Years' War against the English. She was born into a peasant family in the village of Domrémy. By the time she reached the age of 13, much of northern France was in the hands of the English king Henry VI, who had entered into an alliance with the powerful duke of Burgundy. It was then that Joan began to hear voices urging her to drive the English from her home country.

Above: This 19th-century painting shows Joan at the coronation of Charles VII.

SEE ALSO

♦ England
♦ France
♦ Women

Two men had a claim to the French throne—Henry and the dauphin (French heir) Charles, the son of the previous king. Joan presented herself at the dauphin's court in 1429 and managed to convince him of her divine mission to save France. After being approved by the church authorities, she was asked to lead Charles' army to relieve the besieged city of Orléans.

Joan personally led the attack, and her courageous leadership inspired a demoralized army to a series of daring attacks on the English castles surrounding Orléans, which was quickly freed from danger. Emboldened by her victories, Joan persuaded a hesitant Charles to advance on Reims, the city where French kings were traditionally crowned. The French forces inflicted a decisive defeat on the English army along the way at Patay. On July 17, 1429, with Joan by his side, Charles VII was finally anointed king of France in Reims cathedral.

JOAN'S TRIAL AND DEATH

Joan continued to lead the French into battle, but in 1430 she was captured by the forces of the duke of Burgundy, who sold her to the English. Usually, important prisoners were ransomed, but Charles abandoned Joan for political reasons, and she was handed over to a pro-English church court in Rouen. Joan was accused of heresy and after a lengthy interrogation was convicted and burned at the stake on May 30, 1431. A quarter of a century later Joan's case was reopened, and the church found her innocent. She was finally made a saint in 1920.

Julius II

A forceful, plain-speaking man, prone to violent fits of temper, Pope Julius II (1443–1513) was not only the spiritual head of the Catholic church but also a successful military commander and a generous patron of the arts. He commissioned many splendid buildings and great works of art, notably by the painter Raphael, the painter and sculptor Michelangelo, and the architect Bramante.

Julius was born Giuliano delle Rovere in 1443 near Savona, a port on the northwest coast of Italy. He grew up into a determined, physically strong young man and joined the order of Franciscan friars. Although his parents were poor, Giuliano was helped in his church career when his uncle was elected Pope Sixtus IV in 1471. Sixtus immediately made the 28-year-old Giuliano a cardinal and also made him bishop of a number of districts in France and Italy. This brought him much prestige, influence, and wealth.

FROM EXILE TO POPE

Giuliano's fortunes changed for the worse when his old rival and enemy Rodrigo Borgia was elected Pope Alexander VI in 1492. Alexander soon tried to have Giuliano killed. In fear for his life, Giuliano decided to leave Rome and eventually took refuge at the court of Charles VIII, the king of France. He returned to Rome only in 1503. In that year, after the deaths of Alexander and his successor Pius III (who died after reigning for only a month), Giuliano himself was elected pope by his fellow cardinals. He had managed to win

them over with bribes and promises— promises that he never honored.

From the start Julius II—the title Giuliano adopted—was determined to make the papacy strong and independent, able to control its own affairs without outside interference from foreign rulers. He also made it his ambition to reconquer the Papal States —the papacy's own lands. So in 1506 he mounted a military campaign against the cities of Perugia and Bologna, which had declared themselves independent from the papacy, and brought them back under papal control. Then three years later he and

Above: A portrait of Julius II in his old age, copied by Titian from the original painting by Raphael.

Above: The ceiling of the Sistine Chapel in the Vatican. Julius II commissioned Michelangelo to paint it in 1508, and the work took four years. The ceiling measures 118 ft (36m) by 46 ft (14m), and Michelangelo painted it almost entirely himself, without the help of assistants, lying on his back on scaffolding. The design features characters and scenes from the Old Testament.

1512, and after the battle the defeated French retreated beyond the Alps. By the time of his death in the following year Julius had not only achieved his aim of ridding Italy of the French but had also added the cities of Parma and Piacenza to the Papal States.

A GENEROUS PATRON OF THE ARTS

Julius was much more than just a warrior pope. He gained a reputation for being one of the most inspiring and generous patrons of art of the Renaissance. One of the artists he supported was Raphael, whom he hired in 1508 to paint certain rooms in the Vatican Palace, the main residence of the popes. Raphael was ordered to whitewash the existing wall paintings and start afresh. One of the best known of his new creations was a fresco painting called *The School of Athens*. It shows the ancient Greek thinkers Plato and Aristotle discussing ideas as they stroll through a crowd of their followers and other philosophers, some of whom Raphael painted in the likeness of his contemporaries.

THE SISTINE CHAPEL

Another artist patronized by Julius was Michelangelo, whom he commissioned to paint the ceiling of the Vatican's

his allies recovered territories held by the city-state of Venice, so regaining control of the Papal States.

Julius decided next to drive the French, his former allies, out of Italy. In 1511 he joined forces with Venice, Spain, England, and the Holy Roman emperor Maximilian I in an alliance to fight the French. The two opposing armies met at Ravenna on April 11,

 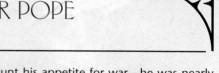

A WARRIOR POPE

Unlike most popes, Julius II was an accomplished military leader who was not afraid to enter battle himself. Known to his contemporaries as *Il terribile*—a name that suggests his energy and ability to inspire awe—Julius personally led the fight to reconquer former papal territories. He was often to be found at the head of his troops, dressed in a suit of shining armor and mounted on a fine horse. Age did not blunt his appetite for war—he was nearly 70 years old when he took charge of the siege of one particular town. He was also physically tough and brave enough to withstand the harshest of weather conditions. On one occasion, for example, he plunged headlong through a snowdrift that rose to the height of his horse's chest and had to shout at his timid companions to follow him.

Left: The tomb of Julius II, carved by Michelangelo, which stands in the church of San Pietro in Vincoli in Rome. The seated figure in the center represents the prophet Moses.

Sistine Chapel. The ceiling took four years to complete and is one of the glories of Western art. It depicts scenes from the Old Testament, including the story of the Creation and Adam and Eve in the garden of Eden. Apart from painters, Julius also commissioned the architect Bramante to refashion Saint Peter's Church—which had originally been constructed by the Roman emperor Constantine in the fourth century A.D. The pope himself laid the foundation stone on April 18, 1506.

Although he is best remembered for his military feats and patronage of the arts, Julius did have some effect on church affairs. He passed measures to stop popes using bribes to get elected, even though he had done so himself. He also organized the Fifth Lateran Council to reform aspects of church practices and appointed bishops to the recently discovered Caribbean islands of Hispaniola and Puerto Rico. And although worldly and ambitious, he attended Mass almost every day.

SEE ALSO
◆ Alexander VI
◆ Bologna
◆ Bramante
◆ Maximilian I
◆ Michelangelo
◆ Papacy
◆ Papal States
◆ Raphael
◆ Rome

Justice and the Law

The Renaissance in Europe was a period when, for many different reasons, the rule of law was under threat. Rising populations put pressure on existing resources, inflation led to an increasing gap between wages and prices, and high levels of taxation were unpopular. All these factors contributed to a general feeling of discontent, which frequently erupted into riots and protests. The challenges to existing authority created by the religious unrest of the Reformation also contributed to the generally violent mood of the times. The legal system—though frequently abused—was the instrument that the authorities used to regulate society and impose order on their unruly subjects.

Left: A 16th-century illustration showing King Louis XI of France sentencing the French noble Charles de Melun to death. The death sentence was the penalty for treason as well as for many lesser crimes.

Above: A detail from a 15th-century painting showing the bodies of two hanged men. This grim sight would not have been unusual in the Renaissance, when the corpses of criminals were often left on display to discourage others from crime.

Throughout the Middle Ages the countries of Europe had evolved their own legal systems. At first they were based on Germanic law, or the laws and customs belonging to the many Germanic tribes that had overrun the Roman Empire. However, toward the end of the Middle Ages the influence of ancient Roman law, codified by the Emperor Justinian in the sixth century A.D., began to permeate legal systems in Europe. In general, civil courts tried crimes against property and person, and were empowered to hand down a severe range of sentences, such as hanging, banishment, imprisonment, and maiming. Clerical courts, presided over by clergymen, dealt with offenses such as blasphemy, irreligion (nonbelief), heresy (belief contrary to the teaching of the church), and marital offenses, such as adultery. They tended to hand out milder punishments, which emphasized public humiliation and repentance, such as enforced public confessions, token fines, and the wearing of penitential garments.

Each country evolved its own body of customary or "common" law. In England judges appointed by the king regularly traveled to regional assizes (courts), where they tried people suspected of serious crimes. The judges were learned men who had studied law at a university and at the Inns of Court in London, and their judgments were based on a growing body of case law, or previous legal cases, known as "precedents." From the 14th century onward juries had begun to evolve. Originally, jurors had been no more than witnesses, who had given sworn testimony at a trial. Gradually, as the legal system became more centralized, juries were called on to actually judge the evidence presented in court. This development replaced earlier modes of trial, such as determining a person's innocence by their ability to withstand physical "ordeals" like branding, when they were burned with hot irons.

LAW AND POWER

The law was an obvious instrument of control and could be used by monarchs to advance and consolidate their power over their subjects. In England the Tudor dynasty began to assert its control by instituting "prerogative" courts, or courts outside of the common law, that took their authority from the supreme power of the monarch. Prerogative courts included the Council of the North and the Council of Wales in the regions where England bordered Scotland and Wales, and the Court of Requests and the

COURT OF STAR CHAMBER

The English Court of Star Chamber developed out of the king's council of advisers of the Middle Ages. It was a court of law that operated in addition to the common law courts and was presided over by judges, peers, and bishops. It was able to deal with cases more quickly and effectively than the common law courts, which were bound by rigid procedures and used juries to reach a verdict. From 1515 the Star Chamber's activities increased under the guidance of Thomas Wolsey (about 1475–1530), King Henry VIII's chancellor, when it became an important means of controlling unruly nobles. The Star Chamber acted vigorously against perjury, slander, forgery, fraud, riots, and any offense against the king or his legislation. It imposed punishments from fines and imprisonment to whipping and mutilation. The Star Chamber was a very powerful body and became increasingly unpopular for its random methods and harsh punishments. It was abolished by Parliament in 1641.

Below: A scene in a 15th-century French court, showing judgment being passed on two criminals. Bound at the neck and wrists, one is led away to his fate—which might be death or mutilation (the loss of a hand or a foot).

Court of Star Chamber. The Court of Requests heard law cases brought by the poor, while the Star Chamber dealt mainly with crimes of forgery, perjury (false testimony), and conspiracy. As Elizabeth I's attorney general (chief law officer), Edward Coke (1552–1664) was a champion of the crown and its prerogative powers, and conducted several famous treason trials. However, as chief justice, he gradually came to resist the power of the monarch and to assert the authority of common law, claiming that the monarch alone should not judge any case.

In France legal institutions reflected an era of expanding territory. As new areas, such as the Dauphiné and Provence, were integrated into the country, they were allowed a measure of local autonomy (self-government) and were permitted to make their own laws. Provinces were granted their own *parlements* (high courts of law): Toulouse in 1443; Grenoble in 1456; Dijon in 1477; Aix in 1501; Rouen in 1515. This state of affairs contributed to a marked local sense of identity, contrasting with England's centralized control of the law.

The violence associated with the religious upheavals in Europe and the conflicts that took place in lands newly discovered by Europeans—such as the Americas—led some legal thinkers like Alberico Gentili (1552–1608) to propose an enforceable international law. This law would be designed to restrain political violence and would be based on the "natural" rights to life and property possessed by all of mankind. However, these revolutionary ideas proved too idealistic, and by the early 17th century legal philosophers were proposing that laws should be devised that dealt with the individual rights of subjects within sovereign nations.

THE LAW OF THE TOWNS

Many Renaissance cities were self-governing, and the lives of their citizens were closely regulated. Town councils, usually chosen from the leading citizens, determined laws to regulate daily life. In crowded, polluted cities laws to control the cleanliness of fountains and drains and to regulate sewage disposal and the location of cesspools, abattoirs, and tanneries (where animal skins were processed into leather using chemicals) were vital. Many cities were blighted by frequent plague epidemics, and a whole series of laws was enacted to try to regulate the spread of disease. In some plague-stricken Italian cities social gatherings were forbidden, houses in which the plague was suspected were sealed (with their unfortunate inhabitants inside), and whole streets were closed off. The authorities decreed when and where funerals could take place. In some cities magistrates even took on the responsibility for policing morals—in Geneva and Augsburg, for example, magistrates had the power to punish quarreling husbands and wives. Fairs,

festivals, and theaters were all closely monitored and banned if they showed signs of getting out of hand. Some cities also passed sumptuary laws, which regulated the clothing that could be worn by different groups of people.

Law enforcement in the towns was the responsibility of a diverse group of people: magistrates, ward (neighborhood) constables, night watchmen, town criers, customs clerks, jailers, and executioners. Perhaps the most effective control was exercised by neighbors. People lived in close proximity, with little privacy. Neighborhoods were responsible for street patrols, watching out for fires, and reporting offenses that ranged from dumping rubbish to harboring criminals. In these close-knit, gossipy communities breaking the law soon became public knowledge.

Above: The death penalty was extremely common in Renaissance times. This late 14th-century scene shows two prisoners being beheaded.

SEE ALSO

♦ Crime and Punishment
♦ Dress
♦ England
♦ France
♦ Henry VIII
♦ Inquisition

Landscape Painting

Above: This landscape was painted by the German artist Albrecht Altdorfer in about 1526–1528. It is one of the earliest examples of a landscape painting in the Renaissance.

Today we are used to seeing paintings of many different subjects. However, before the time of the Renaissance most paintings showed only holy figures or stories from the Bible. In the 15th century artists began to portray these subjects in a more realistic, or lifelike, way and as part of this new approach they started to paint landscapes in the background. Gradually, these land-scape settings were given more prominence, and by the beginning of the 16th century a few artists had begun to produce paintings in which landscape was main subject.

In northern Europe interest in the realistic portrayal of nature grew out of a thriving tradition of manuscript illumination (illustration). From the 13th century northern European paint-ers had produced some of their finest works as decorations to handwritten manuscripts, including calendars and books of hours—which told people the prayers they should say on particular days. These manuscripts were often decorated with pictures of nature and the countryside. They showed scenes of daily life and farming activities that took place at different times of the year, as well as the recreational pursuits of the nobility, such as hunting and falconry.

FLEMISH LANDSCAPES

Outside manuscripts, the first realistic-looking landscapes appeared in the 15th century in the backgrounds of paintings made by artists working in Germany and Flanders (a region that included present-day Belgium and parts of the Netherlands and France). Earlier painters had used either gold leaf for the backgrounds of their pictures or stylized (artificial-looking) landscapes that bore little resemblance to nature. Even the great Italian artist Giotto (about 1267–1337), who is con-sidered the father of the Renaissance, painted artificial-looking landscape backgrounds in his pictures. His

STUDIES OF NATURE

Before the Renaissance, if artists included a landscape setting in their paintings, they usually copied pictures from pattern books, which were like encyclopedias of images. Cennino Cennini, a painter who wrote the only book on painters' methods to survive from medieval times, also advised artists to copy piles of stones if they wanted to create the effect of mountains. It was only in the 15th century that artists started to go out into the countryside to make sketches from nature.

Some of the most famous landscape studies from the period were made by the Italian artist Leonardo da Vinci (1452–1519) and the German artist Albrecht Dürer (1471–1528). Leonardo produced a huge number of pen-and-ink drawings, the subjects of which ranged from plants, woods, fantastic rock formations, and mountains to natural forces such as storms and rivers in torrent. Dürer's landscape studies include many watercolor paintings, such as *View of Arco* (1495), made on a trip to northern Italy.

Studies like these were not intended as finished works of art but as reference material for painting backgrounds in more ambitious pictures. Artists often took elements from different studies in their notebooks and combined them in their finished paintings, and scholars believe that many of the real-

Above: Dürer's View of Arco, *painted in 1495. Dürer was one of the first artists to study landscape and to make landscape sketches as reference material.*

looking backgrounds in Renaissance pictures are actually montages, combining features from many different places that artists saw and sketched.

angular brown rocks and slender trees with huge leaves act as a kind of shorthand for reality.

The same is not true of landscapes by Flemish artists such as Jan van Eyck, Robert Campin, and Hugo van der Goes. Their pictures are characterized by a meticulous attention to detail and a careful observation of appearances. These painters set their religious subjects in the landscapes they saw around them, in the hills, valleys, and fields of northern Europe. The *Ghent Altarpiece* (1432) by Jan and Hubert van Eyck is an early example of a landscape in Flemish painting. It shows the adoration of the lamb (an Old Testament story) set in a brilliant green landscape with carefully drawn plants, rolling hills, and woods that melt into pale blues in the distance.

Van Eyck's successful depiction of landscape and that of his Flemish contemporaries owed much to the development of oil paint. Oil paint was slower drying and more transparent than tempera, which was the paint that had been used before, and it enabled artists to paint intricate details and blend colors seamlessly. By applying oil paint in many thin, almost transparent layers, painters were able to capture the way landscape appears to melt into the distance, becoming increasingly blue the farther away it is—an effect known as "aerial perspective."

Some religious subjects gave artists a greater opportunity to show landscapes than others. One of the most popular subjects in both northern Europe and Italy was the story of Saint Jerome in the wilderness—Jerome retreated to the Syrian desert for four years, where he lived as a hermit. In paintings of this subject the landscape often assumed the same importance as the figure, if not more. This change in emphasis can clearly be seen in the Flemish artist Joachim Patinir's *Landscape with Saint Jerome* painted in about 1520–1524. In the foreground Jerome sits in a cave and tames a lion by removing a thorn from its foot. Other stories from his life are scattered through the picture. The dominant element, however, is the landscape— the huge, jagged rocky outcrops, the rolling green fields and trees, and the blue sea and mountains beyond.

Patinir's paintings influenced many artists in Italy and northern Europe in the 16th century, including Pieter Bruegel the Elder (about 1525–1569). One of Bruegel's most famous works is a series of pictures in which different times of the year are represented by various countryside activities and landscapes. They include people harvesting in golden cornfields, men herding cows in a gloomy brown river valley, and a cold, snowy scene of hunters returning to their village. Bruegel also painted religious and mythological subjects as if they were taking place in the countryside and local villages of his own day.

GERMAN LANDSCAPE PAINTING
Just as landscape played an increasingly important role in Flemish art at the end of the 15th century, so dark wooded settings began to feature in paintings

Left: **Landscape with Saint Jerome** *(about 1520–1524) by Joachim Patinir. While traditional pictures of this subject focused on Saint Jerome, Patinir concentrates on the sweeping landscape setting.*

produced by artists working around the Danube River in Germany. The most famous of these artists are Lucas Cranach (1472–1553) and Albrecht

---

Scholars think that the German painter Albrecht Altdorfer produced the first "pure" landscapes

---

Altdorfer (about 1485–1538). Both painted religious subjects set in dark forests of larch and fir and craggy mountains. Scholars think that Altdorfer produced the first "pure" landscapes—that is, without a human subject—of the Renaissance. His pictures are tiny jewellike works painted in oil paint, with minute attention to detail, deep colors, and a mysterious atmosphere.

THE ITALIAN TRADITION

Italian artists were more concerned with portraying the human figure than landscape. However, despite this trend, some of the earliest surviving examples of landscape painting were made in Italy on the walls of Siena town hall in 1338–1340. They are two pictures by Ambrogio Lorenzetti showing the effects of good and bad government on a town and its surrounding country-side. Lorenzetti captured the dusty browns of the Italian hills and the patterns of the vineyards, although the countryside, particularly the shapes of the trees, looks stylized.

Over a century passed before Italian artists again tackled the depiction of landscape, this time inspired by the example of Flemish painters. From the 1450s Piero della Francesca and the

Pollaiuolo brothers painted realistic views of the countryside around Florence in the backgrounds of their pictures. However, it was in the north Italian city of Venice that a distinctively Italian approach to landscape emerged at the end of the 15th century.

Giovanni Bellini was the first Venetian artist to use landscape settings, and his work influenced Giorgione and Titian. These two painters developed the use of "ideal" or perfected landscapes, which were often based on descriptions by classical authors such as Virgil. They did not show real places but idealized pastures, hills, and trees, which were often bathed in a golden light and populated by shepherds and figures in perfect harmony with their surroundings.

Above: A detail of a 15th-century Italian landscape from a painting by Benozzo Gozzoli.

SEE ALSO

♦ Bellini, Giovanni
♦ Bruegel, Pieter the Elder
♦ Dürer
♦ Eyck, Jan van
♦ Flemish Painting
♦ German Art
♦ Giorgione
♦ Naturalism
♦ Titian

Timeline

- ◆ **1305** Giotto begins work on frescoes for the Arena Chapel, Padua—he is often considered the father of Renaissance art.

- ◆ **1321** Dante publishes the *Divine Comedy*, which has a great influence on later writers.

- ◆ **1327** Petrarch begins writing the sonnets known as the *Canzoniere*.

- ◆ **1337** The start of the Hundred Years' War between England and France.

- ◆ **1353** Boccaccio writes the *Decameron*, an influential collection of 100 short stories.

- ◆ **1368** The Ming dynasty comes to power in China.

- ◆ **1377** Pope Gregory XI moves the papacy back to Rome from Avignon, where it has been based since 1309.

- ◆ **1378** The Great Schism begins: two popes, Urban VI and Clement VII, both lay claim to the papacy.

- ◆ **1378** English theologian John Wycliffe criticizes the practices of the Roman Catholic church.

- ◆ **1380** Ivan I of Muscovy defeats the army of the Mongol Golden Horde at the battle of Kulikovo.

- ◆ **1389** The Ottomans defeat the Serbs at the battle of Kosovo, beginning a new phase of Ottoman expansion.

- ◆ **1397** Sigismund of Hungary is defeated by the Ottoman Turks at the battle of Nicopolis.

- ◆ **1397** Queen Margaret of Denmark unites Denmark, Sweden, and Norway under the Union of Kalmar.

- ◆ **1398** The Mongol leader Tamerlane invades India.

- ◆ **1399** Henry Bolingbroke becomes Henry IV of England.

- ◆ **1400** English writer Geoffrey Chaucer dies, leaving his *Canterbury Tales* unfinished.

- ◆ **1403** In Italy the sculptor Ghiberti wins a competition to design a new set of bronze doors for Florence Cathedral.

- ◆ **c.1402** The Bohemian preacher Jan Hus begins to attack the corruption of the church.

- ◆ **1405** The Chinese admiral Cheng Ho commands the first of seven expeditions to the Indian Ocean and East Africa.

- ◆ **1415** Jan Hus is summoned to the Council of Constance and condemned to death.

- ◆ **1415** Henry V leads the English to victory against the French at the battle of Agincourt.

- ◆ **c.1415** Florentine sculptor Donatello produces his sculpture *Saint George*.

- ◆ **1416** Venice defeats the Ottoman fleet at the battle of Gallipoli, but does not check the Ottoman advance.

- ◆ **1417** The Council of Constance elects Martin V pope, ending the Great Schism.

- ◆ **1418** Brunelleschi designs the dome of Florence Cathedral.

- ◆ **1420** Pope Martin V returns the papacy to Rome, bringing peace and order to the city.

- ◆ **c.1420** Prince Henry of Portugal founds a school of navigation at Sagres, beginning a great age of Portuguese exploration.

- ◆ **1422** Charles VI of France dies, leaving his throne to the English king Henry VI. Charles VI's son also claims the throne.

- ◆ **c.1425** Florentine artist Masaccio paints the *Holy Trinity*, the first painting to use the new science of perspective.

- ◆ **1429** Joan of Arc leads the French to victory at Orléans; Charles VII is crowned king of France in Reims Cathedral.

- ◆ **1431** The English burn Joan of Arc at the stake for heresy.

- ◆ **1433** Sigismund of Luxembourg becomes Holy Roman emperor.

- ◆ **1434** Cosimo de Medici comes to power in Florence.

- ◆ **1434** The Flemish artist Jan van Eyck paints the *Arnolfini Marriage* using the newly developed medium of oil paint.

- ◆ **1439** The Council of Florence proclaims the reunion of the Western and Orthodox churches.

- ◆ **c.1440** Donatello completes his statue of David—the first life-size bronze sculpture since antiquity.

- ◆ **1443** Federigo da Montefeltro becomes ruler of Urbino.

- ◆ **1447** The Milanese people declare their city a republic.

- ◆ **1450** The condottiere Francesco Sforza seizes control of Milan.

- ◆ **1450** Fra Angelico paints *The Annunciation* for the monastery of San Marco in Florence.

- ◆ **1453** Constantinople, capital of the Byzantine Empire, falls to the Ottomans and becomes the capital of the Muslim Empire.

- ◆ **1453** The French defeat the English at the battle of Castillon, ending the Hundred Years' War.

- ◆ **1454–1456** Venice, Milan, Florence, Naples, and the papacy form the Italian League to maintain peace in Italy.

- ◆ **1455** The start of the Wars of the Roses between the Houses of York and Lancaster in England.

- ◆ **c.1455** The German Johannes Gutenberg develops the first printing press using movable type.

- ◆ **1456** The Florentine painter Uccello begins work on the *Battle of San Romano*.

- ◆ **1461** The House of York wins the Wars of the Roses; Edward IV becomes king of England.

- ◆ **1461** Sonni Ali becomes king of the Songhai Empire in Africa.

- ◆ **1462** Marsilio Ficino founds the Platonic Academy of Florence— the birthplace of Renaissance Neoplatonism.

- ◆ **1463** War breaks out between Venice and the Ottoman Empire.

- ◆ **1465** The Italian painter Mantegna begins work on the Camera degli Sposi in Mantua.

- ◆ **1467** Civil war breaks out in Japan, lasting for over a century.

- ◆ **1469** Lorenzo the Magnificent, grandson of Cosimo de Medici, comes to power in Florence.

- ◆ **1469** The marriage of Isabella I of Castile and Ferdinand V of Aragon unites the two kingdoms.

- ◆ **1470** The Florentine sculptor Verrocchio completes his *David*.

- ◆ **1476** William Caxton establishes the first English printing press at Westminster, near London.

- ◆ **1477** Pope Sixtus IV begins building the Sistine Chapel.

- ◆ **c.1477** Florentine painter Sandro Botticelli paints the *Primavera*, one of the first large-scale mythological paintings of the Renaissance.

- ◆ **1478** The Spanish Inquisition is founded in Spain.

- ◆ **1480** The Ottoman fleet destroys the port of Otranto in south Italy.

- ◆ **1485** Henry Tudor becomes Henry VII of England—the start of the Tudor dynasty.

- ◆ **1486** *The Witches' Hammer* is published, a handbook on how to hunt down witches.

- ◆ **1488** Portuguese navigator Bartholomeu Dias reaches the Cape of Good Hope.

- ◆ **1491** Missionaries convert King Nzina Nkowu of the Congo to Christianity.

- ◆ **1492** The Spanish monarchs conquer Granada, the last Moorish territory in Spain.

- ◆ **1492** Christopher Columbus lands in the Bahamas, claiming the territory for Spain.

- ◆ **1492** Henry VII of England renounces all English claims to the French throne.

- ◆ **1493** The Hapsburg Maximilian becomes Holy Roman emperor.

- ◆ **1494** Charles VIII of France invades Italy, beginning four decades of Italian wars.

- ◆ **1494** In Italy Savonarola comes to power in Florence.

- ◆ **1494** The Treaty of Tordesillas divides the non-Christian world between Spain and Portugal.

- ◆ **1495** Leonardo da Vinci begins work on *The Last Supper* .

- ◆ **1495** Spain forms a Holy League with the Holy Roman emperor and expels the French from Naples.

- ◆ **1498** Portuguese navigator Vasco da Gama reaches Calicut, India.

- ◆ **1498** German artist Dürer creates the *Apocalypse* woodcuts.

- ◆ **1500** Portuguese navigator Pedro Cabral discovers Brazil.

- ◆ **c.1500–1510** Dutch painter Hieronymous Bosch paints *The Garden of Earthly Delights*.

- ◆ **c.1502** Italian architect Donato Bramante designs the Tempietto Church in Rome.

- ◆ **1503** Leonardo da Vinci begins painting the *Mona Lisa*.

- ◆ **1504** Michelangelo finishes his statue of David, widely seen as a symbol of Florence.

- ◆ **c.1505** Venetian artist Giorgione paints *The Tempest*.

♦ **1506** The Italian architect Donato Bramante begins work on rebuilding Saint Peter's, Rome.

♦ **1508** Michelangelo begins work on the ceiling of the Sistine Chapel in the Vatican.

♦ **1509** Henry VIII ascends the throne of England.

♦ **1509** The League of Cambrai defeats Venice at the battle of Agnadello.

♦ **1510–1511** Raphael paints *The School of Athens* in the Vatican.

♦ **1511** The French are defeated at the battle of Ravenna in Italy and are forced to retreat over the Alps.

♦ **1513** Giovanni de Medici becomes Pope Leo X.

♦ **1515** Thomas Wolsey becomes lord chancellor of England.

♦ **1515** Francis I becomes king of France. He invades Italy and captures Milan.

♦ **c.1515** German artist Grünewald paints the *Isenheim Altarpiece*.

♦ **1516** Charles, grandson of the emperor Maximilian I, inherits the Spanish throne as Charles I.

♦ **1516** Thomas More publishes his political satire *Utopia*.

♦ **1516** Dutch humanist Erasmus publishes a more accurate version of the Greek New Testament.

♦ **1517** Martin Luther pins his 95 theses on the door of the castle church in Wittenburg.

♦ **1519** Charles I of Spain becomes Holy Roman emperor Charles V.

♦ **1519–1521** Hernán Cortés conquers Mexico for Spain.

♦ **1520** Henry VIII of England and Francis I of France meet at the Field of the Cloth of Gold to sign a treaty of friendship.

♦ **1520** Portuguese navigator Ferdinand Magellan discovers a route to the Indies around the tip of South America.

♦ **1520** Süleyman the Magnificent becomes ruler of the Ottoman Empire, which now dominates the eastern Mediterranean.

♦ **1520–1523** Titian paints *Bacchus and Ariadne* for Alfonso d'Este.

♦ **1521** Pope Leo X excommuicates Martin Luther.

♦ **1521** The emperor Charles V attacks France, beginning a long period of European war.

♦ **1522** Ferdinand Magellan's ship the *Victoria* is the first to sail around the world.

♦ **1523–1525** Huldrych Zwingli sets up a Protestant church at Zurich in Switzerland.

♦ **1525** In Germany the Peasants' Revolt is crushed, and its leader, Thomas Münzer, is executed.

♦ **1525** The emperor Charles V defeats the French at the battle of Pavia and takes Francis I prisoner.

♦ **1525** William Tyndale translates the New Testament into English.

♦ **1526** The Ottoman Süleyman the Magnificent defeats Hungary at the battle of Mohács.

♦ **1526** Muslim Mongol leader Babur invades northern India and establishes the Mogul Empire.

♦ **c.1526** The Italian artist Correggio paints the *Assumption of the Virgin* in Parma Cathedral.

♦ **1527** Charles V's armies overrun Italy and sack Rome.

♦ **1527–1530** Gustavus I founds a Lutheran state church in Sweden.

♦ **1528** Italian poet and humanist Baldassare Castiglione publishes *The Courtier*.

♦ **1529** The Ottoman Süleyman the Magnificent lays siege to Vienna, but eventually retreats.

♦ **1530** The Catholic church issues the "Confutation," attacking Luther and Protestantism.

♦ **1531** The Protestant princes of Germany form the Schmalkaldic League.

♦ **1531–1532** Francisco Pizarro conquers Peru for Spain.

♦ **1532** Machiavelli's *The Prince* is published after his death.

♦ **1533** Henry VIII of England rejects the authority of the pope and marries Anne Boleyn.

♦ **1533** Anabaptists take over the city of Münster in Germany.

♦ **1533** Christian III of Denmark founds the Lutheran church of Denmark.

♦ **1534** Paul III becomes pope and encourages the growth of new religious orders such as the Jesuits.

♦ **1534** Luther publishes his German translation of the Bible.

♦ **1534** The Act of Supremacy declares Henry VIII supreme head of the Church of England.

♦ **c.1535** Parmigianino paints the mannerist masterpiece *Madonna of the Long Neck*.

♦ **1535–1536** The Swiss city of Geneva becomes Protestant and expels the Catholic clergy.

♦ **1536** Calvin publishes *Institutes of the Christian Religion*, which sets out his idea of predestination.

♦ **1536** Pope Paul III sets up a reform commission to examine the state of the Catholic church.

♦ **1537** Hans Holbein is appointed court painter to Henry VIII of England.

♦ **1539** Italian painter Bronzino begins working for Cosimo de Medici the Younger in Florence.

♦ **1539** Ignatius de Loyola founds the Society of Jesus (the Jesuits).

♦ **1541** John Calvin sets up a model Christian city in Geneva.

♦ **1543** Andreas Vesalius publishes *On the Structure of the Human Body*, a handbook of anatomy based on dissections.

♦ **1543** Polish astronomer Copernicus's *On the Revolutions of the Heavenly Spheres* proposes a sun-centered universe.

♦ **1544** Charles V and Francis I of France sign the Truce of Crespy.

♦ **1545** Pope Paul III organizes the Council of Trent to counter the threat of Protestantism.

♦ **1545** Spanish explorers find huge deposits of silver in the Andes Mountains of Peru.

♦ **1547** Charles V defeats the Protestant Schmalkaldic League at the Battle of Mühlberg.

♦ **1547** Ivan IV "the Terrible" declares himself czar of Russia.

♦ **1548** Titian paints the equestrian portrait *Charles V after the Battle of Mühlberg*.

♦ **1548** Tintoretto paints *Saint Mark Rescuing the Slave*.

♦ **1550** Italian Georgio Vasari publishes his *Lives of the Artists*.

♦ **1553** Mary I of England restores the Catholic church.

♦ **1554** Work begins on the Cathedral of Saint Basil in Red Square, Moscow.

♦ **1555** At the Peace of Augsburg Charles V allows the German princes to determine their subjects' religion.

♦ **1556** Ivan IV defeats the last Mongol khanates. Muscovy now dominates the Volga region.

♦ **1556** Philip II becomes king of Spain.

♦ **1559** Elizabeth I of England restores the Protestant church.

♦ **1562** The Wars of Religion break out in France.

♦ **1565** Flemish artist Pieter Bruegel the Elder paints *Hunters in the Snow*.

♦ **1565** Italian architect Palladio designs the Villa Rotunda, near Vicenza.

♦ **1566** The Dutch revolt against the Spanish over the loss of political and religious freedoms;

Philip II of Spain sends 10,000 troops under the duke of Alba to suppress the revolt.

♦ **1569** Flemish cartographer Mercator produces a world map using a new projection.

♦ **1571** Philip II of Spain and an allied European force defeat the Ottomans at the battle of Lepanto.

♦ **1572** In Paris, France, a Catholic mob murders thousands of Huguenots in the Saint Bartholomew's Day Massacre.

♦ **1572** Danish astronomer Tycho Brahe sees a new star.

♦ **1573** Venetian artist Veronese paints the *Feast of the House of Levi*.

♦ **1579** The seven northern provinces of the Netherlands form the Union of Utrecht.

♦ **1580** Giambologna creates his mannerist masterpiece *Flying Mercury*.

♦ **1585** Henry III of France bans Protestantism in France; civil war breaks out again in the War of the Three Henrys.

♦ **1586** El Greco, a Greek artist active in Spain, paints the *Burial of Count Orgaz*.

♦ **1587** Mary, Queen of Scots, is executed by Elizabeth I of England.

♦ **c.1587** Nicholas Hilliard paints the miniature *Young Man among Roses*.

♦ **1588** Philip II of Spain launches his great Armada against England —but the fleet is destroyed.

♦ **1589** Henry of Navarre becomes king of France as Henry IV.

♦ **1592–1594** Tintoretto paints *The Last Supper*.

♦ **1596** Edmund Spencer publishes the *Faerie Queene*, glorifying Elizabeth I as "Gloriana."

♦ **1598** Henry IV of France grants Huguenots and Catholics equal political rights.

♦ **1598** In England the Globe Theater is built on London's south bank; it stages many of Shakespeare's plays.

♦ **1600–1601** Caravaggio paints *The Crucifixion of Saint Peter*, an early masterpiece of baroque art.

♦ **1603** Elizabeth I of England dies and is succeeded by James I, son of Mary, Queen of Scots.

♦ **1610** Galileo's *The Starry Messenger* supports the sun-centered model of the universe.

♦ **1620** The Italian painter Artemisia Gentileschi paints *Judith and Holofernes*.

Glossary

A.D. The letters A.D. stand for the Latin Anno Domini which means "in the year of our Lord." Dates with these letters written after them are measured forward from the year Christ was born.

Altarpiece A painting or sculpture placed behind an altar in a church.

Apprentice Someone (usually a young person) legally bound to a craftsman for a number of years in order to learn a craft.

Baptistery Part of a church, or a separate building, where people are baptized.

B.C. Short for "Before Christ." Dates with these letters after them are measured backward from the year of Christ's birth.

Bureaucracy A system of government that relies on a body of officials and usually involves much paperwork and many regulations.

Classical A term used to describe the civilizations of ancient Greece and Rome, and any later art and architecture based on ancient Greek and Roman examples.

Commission To order a specially made object, like a painting or tapestry.

Condottiere A mercenary soldier, that is, a soldier who will fight for anyone in return for money.

Contemporary Someone or something that lives or exists at the same period of time.

Diet A general assembly of representatives of the Holy Roman Empire who gathered to pass laws and make decisions.

Edict A proclamation or order that has the force of law.

Envoy Someone sent abroad to represent a ruler or government.

Excommunicate To ban someone from taking part in the rites of the church.

Foreshortening A technique used by artists in their pictures to recreate the appearance of objects when seen from a particular angle. It involves shortening some measurements, according to the laws of perspective (see below), to make it look as if objects are projecting toward or receding away from the surface of the picture.

Fresco A type of painting that is usually used for decorating walls and ceilings in which colors are painted into wet plaster.

Guild An association of merchants or craftsmen organized to protect the interests of its members and to regulate the quality of their goods and services.

Heresy A belief that is contrary to the accepted teachings of the church.

Heretic Someone whose beliefs contradict the teachings of the church.

Humanism A new way of thinking about human life that characterized the Renaissance. It was based on the study of "humanities"— that is, ancient Greek and Roman texts, history, and philosophy—and stressed the importance of developing rounded, cultured people.

Hundred Years' War A long-drawn-out war between France and England, lasting from 1337 to 1453. It consisted of a series of campaigns with periods of tense peace in between.

Indulgences Cancelations of punishments for sins. Indulgences were often granted by the church in return for money.

Laity or lay people Anyone who is not of the clergy.

Low Countries A region in Europe bordering the North Sea and comprising present-day Belgium, Luxembourg, and the Netherlands.

Motif A repeated element in a design.

Municipality A town or city that is an independent political unit with self-governing status.

Mural A painting on a wall. In the Renaissance murals were used to decorate the inside of rooms as well as the outside walls of houses.

Orders A term used in classical architecture for the five different types of classical columns and the rules governing their use.

Patron Someone who orders and pays for a work of art.

Patronage The act of ordering and paying for a work of art.

Perspective A technique that allows artists to create the impression of three-dimensional space in their pictures. Near objects are made to appear larger, and distant objects are shown as smaller.

Piecework Work that is paid for according to the amount done (rather than according to the time it has taken).

Sarcophagus A stone coffin, often decorated with carved side panels.

Siege A military blockade of a castle or a town to force it to surrender, often by cutting off its supplies of food and water.

Tempera A type of paint made by mixing powdered pigments (colors) with egg. It was widely used in medieval times and the Renaissance.

Theology The study of religion, including faith, practice, and experience.

Treason The name given to a subject's act of betrayal of their king or queen.

Treatise A book or long essay about the principles, or rules, of a particular subject.

Triptych A picture or carving consisting of three panels side by side. It was often used as an altarpiece.

Vassal A person who is bound to a local lord to whom they owe their loyalty and services.

Vatican The headquarters of the pope and papal government in Rome.

Vernacular The language of the ordinary people of a country, rather than a literary or formal language such as Latin.

Further Reading

Airs, Malcolm. *The Tudor and Jacobean Country House: A Building History*. Stroud, UK: Sutton Publishing, 1997.

Anderson, James Maxwell. *Daily Life during the Spanish Inquisition*. Westport, CT: Greenwood Publishing, 2002.

Armstrong, Karen. *Islam: A Short History*. New York: Modern Library, 2000.

Batschman, Oskar. *Hans Holbein*. Princeton, NJ: Princeton University Press, 1997.

Berinstain, Valerie. *India and the Mughal Dynasty*. New York: Harry N. Abrams, 1998.

Bloom, Jonathan, and Sheila Blair. *Islam: A Thousand Years of Faith and Power*. New Haven, CT: Yale University Press, 2001.

Burke, Peter. *The Italian Renaissance*. Princeton, NJ: Princeton University Press, 1999.

Crankshaw, Edward. *The Habsburgs: Portrait of a Dynasty*. New York: Viking Press, 1971.

Dean, Trevor. *Crime, Society and the Law in Renaissance Italy*. Cambridge. UK: Cambridge University Press, 1994.

Delay, Nelly. *The Art and Culture of Japan*. New York: Harry N. Abrams, 1999.

Di Cagno, Gabriella. *Michelangelo*. New York: Peter Bedrick Books, 2000.

Dwyer, Freank. *Henry VIII*. Broomall, PA: Chelsea House Publishers, 1988.

Editors of Time-Life Books. *What Life Was Like among Samurai and Shoguns*. Alexandria, VA: Time-Life Books, 2000.

Editors of Time-Life Books. *What Life Was Like at the Rebirth of Genius: Renaissance Italy, AD 1400–1550*. Alexandria, VA: Time-Life Books, 1999.

Edwards, John. *The Jews in Western Europe 1400–1600*. Manchester, UK: Manchester University Press, 1995.

Gordon, Matthew. *Islam*. New York: Facts on File, 1991.

Grant, Neil. *Guilds*. New York: Franklin Watts, 1972.

Green, Robert. *King Henry VIII*. New York: Franklin Watts, 1998.

Greengrass, Mark. *The Longman Companion to the European Reformation, c.1500–1618*. Reading, MA: Addison-Wesley Publishing, 1998.

Harris, Nathaniel. *Leonardo and the Renaissance*. New York: Bookwright Press, 1987.

Hartt, Frederick. *History of Italian Renaissance Art: Painting, Sculpture, Architecture*. New York: Harry N. Abrams, 1994.

Heer, Friedrich. *The Holy Roman Empire*. London: Weidenfeld & Nicolson, 1968.

Hillenbrand, Robert. *Islamic Art and Architecture*. London: Thames & Hudson, 1998.

Icher, Francois. *The Artisans and Guilds of France: Beautiful Craftsmanship through the Centuries*. New York: Harry N. Abrams, 2000.

Irwin, Robert. *Islamic Art in Context: Art, Architecture, and the Literary World*. New York: Harry N. Abrams, 1997.

Keay, John. *India: A History*. New York: Grove Press, 2001.

Mack, Rosamond E. *Bazaar to Piazza: Islamic Trade and Italian Art, 1300–1600*. Berkeley, CA: University of California Press, 2001.

MacKenney, Richard. *Tradesmen and Traders: The World of the Guilds in Venice and Europe, c.1250–1650*. London: Routledge, 1990.

Mitchell, George, Ernst J. Grube, James Dickie, and Oleg Grabar. *Architecture of the Islamic World: Its History and Social Meaning*. London: Thames & Hudson, 1995.

O'Malley, John W. *The First Jesuits*. Cambridge, MA: Harvard University Press, 1995.

Olin, John C. *The Catholic Reformation: Savonarola to Ignatius Loyola*. New York: Fordham University Press, 1993.

Peters, Edward M. *Inquisition*. Berkeley, CA: University of California Press, 1988.

Pettit, Jayne. *Michelangelo: Genius of the Renaissance*. New York: Franklin Watts, 1998.

Pilbeam, Mavis. *Japan under the Shoguns, 1185–1868*. Austin, TX: Raintree/Steck Vaughn, 1999.

Rutter, Jill. *Jewish Migrations*. New York: Thomson Learning, 1995.

Saint-Saens, Alain. *Young Charles V, 1500–1531*. New Orleans, LA: University Press of the South, 2000.

Shaw, Christine. *Julius II: The Warrior Pope*. Oxford: Blackwell Publishers, 1993.

Smith, Robert Sidney. *The Spanish Guild Merchant*. New York, Octagon Books, 1972.

Stanley, Diane. *Leonardo da Vinci*. New York: HarperTrophy, 2000.

Stanley, Diane. *Michelangelo*. New York: HarperCollins Children's Books, 2000.

Stein, Burton. *A History of India*. Oxford: Blackwell Publishers, 1998.

Stewart, Gail B. *Life during the Spanish Inquisition*. San Diego, CA: Lucent Books, 1998.

Swan, Erin Pembrey. *India*. New York: Children's Press, 2002.

Weir, Alison. *Henry VIII: The King and His Court*. New York: Ballantine Books, 2001.

Welch, Stuart Cary. *India: Art and Culture 1300–1900*. New York: Holt, Rinehart, & Winston, 1985.

Wilson, Derek. *Hans Holbein*. London: Weidenfeld & Nicolson, 1996.

Wilson, Peter H. *The Holy Roman Empire 1495–1806*. New York: St. Martin's Press. 1999.

WEBSITES

World history site
www.historyworld.net

BBC Online: History
www.bbc.co.uk/history

The Webmuseum's tour of the Renaissance
www.oir.ucf.edu/wm/paint/glo/renaissance/

Virtual time travel tour of the Renaissance
library.thinkquest.org/3588/Renaissance/

The Renaissance
www.learner.org/exhibits/renaissance

National Gallery of Art—tour of 16th-century Italian paintings
www.nga.gov/collection/gallery/ita16.htm

Uffizi Art Gallery, Florence
musa.uffizi.firenze.it/welcomeE.html

Database of Renaissance artists
www.artcyclopedia.com/index.html

Set Index

Numbers in **bold type** are volume numbers.

Page numbers in *italics* refer to pictures or their captions.

Picture Credits

Cover: AKG London/S Domingie/M Rabatti; title page: The Art Archive.
Pages: 4 Sonia Halliday Photographs/Laura Lushington; 5 Corbis/Gianni Dagli
Orti; 6 AKG London/Cameraphoto; 7 AKG London/S Domingie/M Rabatti; 8 AKG
London/Erich Lessing; 9 Corbis/Tim Thompson; 10 The Art Archive/Dagli Orti;
11 Scala/Civic Museum, Bologna; 12 The Art Archive/Dagli Orti; 13 The
Bridgeman Art Library/Hever Castle; 14 Scala; 15 The Bridgeman Art Library;
16 Corbis/Francis G Mayer; 17 The Art Archive; 18 AKG London; 19 The Art
Archive/Dagli Orti; 21 AKG London/Erich Lessing; 22 Ancient Art &
Architecture; 23 The Art Archive/Dagli Orti; 24 The Art Archive/Dagli Orti; 25 AKG London/
Cameraphoto; 26 Scala/Borghese Gallery; 27 AKG London/Rabatti/S Domingie;
28 Scala/Laurentian Library; 29 The Art Archive/Dagli Orti; 30 The Art Archive/
Dagli Orti; 31 AKG London/S Domingie; 32 AKG London; 33 Corbis/Angelo
Hornak; 34 Corbis/Abbie Enock/Travel Ink; 36 The Art Archive/V&A London;
37 AKG London/Erich Lessing; 38 Mary Evans Picture Library/Hans Burgkmair;
39 The Art Archive; 40 The Art Archive/Dagli Orti; 41 Corbis/Charles & Josette
Lenars; 42 The Bridgeman Art Library/Louvre; 43 AKG London/Orsi Battaglini;
44 Corbis/Aisa; 46–47 Scala/Uffizi Gallery; 48–52 The Art Archive/Dagli Orti;
53 The Art Archive/British Library; 54 Scala; 55 The Art Archive; 56–57 The Art
Archive/Dagli Orti; 58–59 Scala; 60 AKG London; 61 The Art Archive/Dagli Orti;
62 Mary Evans Picture Library; 63 Peter Newark's Pictures; 64 Scala/Alte
Pinakothek, Munich; 65 AKG London; 66 The Bridgeman Art Library/Prado
Museum; 67 AKG London/Erich Lessing.

MAPS

The maps in this book show the locations of cities, states, and empires of the
Renaissance period. However, for the sake of clarity, present-day place names are
often used.